Tears are words that need to be written

Paulo Coelho

What people are saying

We often admire the actions of superheroes and gods, but Mary's story is even more compelling than those fables because she showed us that we do not need heroes to save us, that even without magical abilities, we alone can win over an injustice that for decades seemed all-powerful and unbeatable.

With no superpowers, Mary stood up to evil so great that it enslaved her mother for life. I cannot imagine the amount of courage it took to do so. In turn, she empowers us and more, she keeps fighting for those too young or too beaten to resist.

Dear Mary, I am profoundly grateful that you shared your story so that the rest of us could have a guiding light. You are a pillar of strength. Not because you seem impermeable to suffering and pain, on the contrary, but because no matter how much life put you through, you faced it head on and through all that pain, you kept fighting. You are one of the reasons I don't give up.

Dr. Gabriela Novak

A story of courage, forgiveness, and brutal honesty. Also a terrifying story of pain, deception and manipulation, which at times makes the heart break.

Mary's story shows us so many facets of life, and so many ways in which we can either be destroyed by oppression or rise up against it and fight back. Not everyone has the courage, strength or opportunity to do so, and this makes the voice of those who do even more important. By speaking up about the unspeakable, Mary is a voice not only for herself but also for countless other victims and survivors of child sexual abuse.

Mary's story also forces us to realise that there were many missed opportunities and lost occasions to understand that something was seriously wrong in the house where she and her family lived. As a professional in the field of children's rights and child protection, to me this pinpoints a staggering flaw in the system: the absence of communication and cooperation between different sectors – be it the justice, the social welfare, or the health sector.

By not communicating across sectors, the system contributes inadvertently to exacerbating already extremely grave situations, allowing abusive circumstances to persist and, in the worst cases, even putting lives in peril. This is not a fatality, and it is up to us to find better solutions by which a multi-sectorial and interdisciplinary way of working is more than a matter of chance and becomes a systematic and integrated approach to child protection.

Dr. Susanna Greijer (PhD)
Research, Legal and Policy Consultant
Children's rights and protection of children from violence

This book has stirred up a lot of things in me, whether they are memories that were deliberately or unconsciously repressed or events that were fully experienced. In this sense, Mary and I have a lot in common. This does not prevent us from having our differences, each of us having gone through the trials in our own way. But that is the beauty of diversity. It is also this diversity that makes us strong, we who are called 'victims' but who - in fact - are warriors. By fighting various battles to get out of the quagmires, we have become fighters.

I join Mary in her fight against sexual abuse and various forms of abuse of children. By nature, a child fully trusts adults. It is therefore up to us/you as adults, whether as a parent, family member, neighbor, teacher, doctor, or any other close (or not) person to provide them with a reassuring framework, a framework in which they are not afraid to express themselves. It is essential to free speech, to break the chains of taboos and unsaid things. Certainly, it is difficult to accuse one's own parents, as Mary courageously did.

But it is necessary, even vital, to break these chains. Together we will succeed!
The more of us who speak out, who come out of our dusty closets, the more we will be listened to and the more we will be heard (I also use the masculine, because sexual abuse and other forms of abuse do not only concern girls).

I agree with Mary when she says that if anyone should be ashamed, it is the perpetrator himself, be it in the case of harassment, any form of violence, rape or sexual abuse. It is up to us to be proud to stand up and fight it!

Thank you Mary for opening our eyes and giving us the courage to fight again and again.

Katia, a resilient survivor after sexual abuse from age 10 to 17, a professional burnout at 44, and cancer (followed by lifelong disabilities) at 53.

TEDx Luxembourg City 2021

'Suffering is very subjective. My hell may not be your hell and yet, it may cause you to experience an equal level of distress' proclaims Dr. Mary Faltz in her profound talk. Walking us through her turbulent life path, she highlights the magic of resilience, self-discovery, kindness, and gratitude. Regardless of the adversity, this powerful talk will encourage you to explore happiness after hell in a different light.

Watch the full TEDx talk here!

A WORD FROM THE AUTHOR

What kind of person endlessly hurts people whilst enjoying absolute impunity? Is that infliction of pain spontaneous, opportunistic, or strategic? In this work, I am set to find the answers to my infinite questions. Most likely, I will never be able to fully comprehend the WHY but I am more than determined to expose the HOW in the following pages through extensive digging in the grim past.

Being a researcher, my curious nature observes, investigates, and analyses to draw conclusions. Driven by the revelations of the past weeks, I find myself pushed to write, nearly unconsciously, as I have done it before. I don't know why my mother's recent death triggered me to start typing again but it seems that the overwhelming feeling of injustice and in this case, the injustice towards my mother was a prerequisite. Writing is undoubtedly very therapeutic for me as I have seen first-hand when I wrote my first book in the fear of death while undergoing heavy cancer treatment. I also realise, however, that by writing and publishing, I am giving a voice to the voiceless.

This includes every human being who has had to face any form of violence, be it physical, psychological, or sexual. Through my words, I am finally giving my mother a voice. A voice she was never able to use and even though I can't physically save her anymore, I am certain that she is watching over me with a smile. I can feel that she is proud of me for standing up for what is morally right against all repercussions that arise due to me uncovering the painful truth.

Her honour and dignity will be restored through the pages while my children will always have access to the absolute truth in a tangible form. Growing up, they should never feel the need to look for the answers themselves only because the reality is too cruel to put into words; honest and open communication is the only way forward.

There are many reasons why people read my words. Many have been a victim at some point, others have a genuine curiosity in the topic while some have hurt me in the past and so, with a pounding heart and sweaty palms, they are the first ones to buy my books. Before even exiting the bookstore, they nervously screen the pages to check whether they appear in my narrative. You know who you are and thank you for your purchase.

Regardless of the reason for holding this book between your hands right now, I hope that you find the answers that may help you complete or modulate your own puzzle. It wasn't until two weeks ago that I came to the realisation that when it comes to my mother, my puzzle had been falsified by my abuser over the past 30 years.

Better late than never, I am very thankful to be alive today after a horrid cancer journey to finally restore my puzzle that was incomplete while many pieces were wrongly put together and others had their tabs cut on purpose. This book is merely a snapshot of the hell my mother went through in harrowing silence.

With each page that I filled, the love, respect, and empathy for my mother have only grown stronger and so have the tears, sadness, and regret of not having been armed with the truth sooner. The parallels between both our ordeals have been blatantly staring at me for some time but it's only now that I realise that she loved me and did her best to protect me from evil.

I love you, Mama.
Mary

DEDICATION

This book is dedicated to my beautiful mother Dr. Nora Shaghory – may her soul rest in eternal peace and may she regain her stolen dignity and honour through these writings.

To my sweet children Quentin, Philip, Oliver, Nina, and Alexander – may you always hold the ultimate truth of my family history, however painful it may be for you to discover.

ACKNOWLEDGEMENTS

To my sweet children; you give me superhuman strength to move mountains, time and time again. The past few years have been extremely difficult and I am forever grateful to have had all of you by my side to remind me that all this suffering was not in vain. Thank you for being you, I love you so much!

To those who have been supportive over the past years; you will recognise yourselves. Thank you!

To the competent medical team who saved my life after my cancer diagnosis; to the lovely nurses who were gentle with me and my veins; to the kind secretaries who were patient and understanding, receiving my continuous requests – Thank you!

To my amazing SCRIPT family; you adopted me unconditionally and make work not feel like work – Thank you for the fantastic 18 months so far, to many many more!

My Father

by
Mary Faltz

Published by
Filament Publishing Ltd
14, Croydon Road, Beddington,
Croydon , Surrey CR0 4PA
+44(0)20 8688 2698
www.filamentpublishing.com

My Father
© 2023 Mary Faltz

ISBN 978-1-915465-28-3

The right to be recognised as the author of this work has been asserted by Mary Faltz in accordance with the Designs and Copyrights Act 1988 Section 77

All rights reserved
No part of this work may by copied without the prior written permission of the publishers

Printed by 4Edge
Proofread by Amira Elbanna
Photo Credits: Cover – Massen Photography
Page 6 – Marcela Hernoux
Page 7 - Gretel F&G Photography

Disclaimer
Some names have been changed to protect the privacy of individuals. The events in this book are not fictional but are entirely based on a true story. This book contains no medical recommendations.

Contents

	Preface	16
1	The Aftermath	18
2	The Quest	41
3	The Diagnosis	67
4	The Hospital Ward	97
5	His Mask	119
6	His Cruelty	136
7	The Criminal Investigation	160
8	His Criminal Trial	191
9	His Present	213
10	My Verdict	232
	Glossary of medical terms	256
	Useful contacts	260

Preface

With this second book, Mary Faltz takes us even deeper into the nightmare of her life, risking eliciting from her readers reactions of rejection or even disbelief in this disturbing reality.

For me, the story that Mary shares with us is on par with that of a family living under a dictatorship. Everything is mixed in: physical and psychological violence, manipulation, disinformation, the invention of a family myth, brainwashing, threats... As a result, everyone is a victim, forced to react or endure, and an avalanche of reactions risks causing even more misfortune. How can we help everyone to stop this cycle, calm their emotions, and live a more peaceful future?

I dare to hope that this book will be therapeutic for Mary. I invite the reader to show a lot of indulgence towards her outbursts, to understand her rage, and to share a part of her suffering. This book is a plea for the prosecution, and how could it be otherwise for a victim who continues to be attacked, who discovers the suffering of her mother, and who endures the reactions of her brothers and sisters, who themselves are caught up in a story that is beyond them.

For people of goodwill, be they close to the victim, therapists, decision-makers, it is a matter of reacting, of allowing people to evolve, to change, and of supporting those who engage in this path. Changing one's attitude is one of the most difficult human tasks to achieve. One of the most promising paths for this perilous adventure is prevention, working with our children. It is in this endeavour that Mary is now committed, and I admire her courage and enthusiasm in pursuing this project.

Dr. Roland Seligmann
Leading Paediatrician / Founder and President of the *Association Luxembourgeoise de Pédiatrie Sociale* (ALUPSE) created in 1984, a crucial actor in the prevention of child abuse as well as the therapeutic care of children and young people in Luxembourg

Chapter One

The Aftermath

Sitting in the tiny cubicle, wearing nothing but a yellow hospital gown made of a scratchy light material, my heart is pounding at full throttle. I am waiting, yet again. It seemed I had spent most of the past two years waiting. Waiting to see my doctor, waiting for a scan, for a result, for an appointment. Waiting for approval, for a prescription, for a letter, call, or email. The waiting has seemed never-ending at times. Coupled with anxious anticipation, I nearly got used to this waiting game. I knew that this was and had become part of the deal since my cancer diagnosis two years earlier. A brutal diagnosis that changed my life when my youngest child was only one year old.

'Mrs. Faltz?' – the voice of the radiologist sounds calm, yet serious. A middle-aged man in a white coat enters the little space. There's barely enough room for both of us. My heart stops, the knot in my stomach tightens and I stand up. Expecting the worst as that is how I have been conditioned all my life, I try to remain as calm as possible. I do my best to stay in the present moment. The past two years have caused me to frequently dissociate once the information becomes too heavy to handle. A dissociation between body and mind, which was crucial for survival. 'Everything is fine', continues the kind voice and the radiologist casually walks out of the compact cabin. Still detached from my body, I let out a smiley 'Thank you very much!', which is fortunately still caught by the man in white on his way out. As in a trance state, I put my pretty blue dress, black boots, and classy yellow coat back on before heading to the waiting room.

There, I can continue waiting, this time for a CD and if I'm lucky enough, a report of the scan. In disbelief of the good news, while being set on bad news, I continue staring into the emptiness in the dull waiting area. Waiting rooms come in all shapes and colours. All of them, however, bear the same aura of lethargy, anxiety, and relief. With the recent (still ongoing) pandemic, the imposed social distance has caused random human connections to be a scarce occurrence. And so, people-watching has become one of my favourite activities. Thankfully the mask helps with discretion. Looking around, I spot an elderly man laughing and seemingly relaxed, waiting for his routine appointment, accompanied by a relative.

On the other side of the room sits a young couple, looking anxious while putting on a brave face, playing with their happy blonde toddler sitting in a blue pushchair. Judging by the hospital bracelet, I can only assume that the young father is waiting for his turn to enter the scanning facility because of a new suspicious mass or a cancer follow-up scan like mine. It can also be something completely different but serious, it seems.

Solely basing my assumptions on body language, I make up stories of these random people around me. This definitely makes the endless waiting feel shorter. I quickly remind myself, however, not to judge these people based on what I see as appearances can be very deceiving and I love calling out that particular flaw of society in public. Who knows, maybe that elderly man is terminally ill and laughs with his relative to distract himself from his harsh reality? Perhaps, the young father is only in that waiting room for a routine scan to follow up on his broken ankle post-football game? Perhaps, he and his wife look nervous because they had received an unexpectedly high gas bill that morning? Perhaps, the woman is not even his wife, but his sister, what do I know? Again, I remind myself, never to assume.

While it will take some time to fully come down from my anticipated worst-case scenario to the present and real best-case scenario, I am slowly reconnecting my body and mind to begin to feel the overflowing gratitude of being told that I am allowed to live on. I smile behind my mask at other patients in the waiting room as I can barely keep the news of the good scan to myself.

Once reconnected, I immediately text Catia first to share my joy. 'Everything is clean, I am crying, I was so scared!' my message reads. 'How wonderful!!!! I am so happy for you!' she swiftly replies. I leave the hospital with a huge smile. Grinning at every person I pass, some smile back but most either just find me strange and suspicious or are simply too immersed in their mobile phones to notice me. I console myself and acknowledge that society has sadly evolved into people being more and more connected, yet totally disconnected. What an absolute paradox, I think and walk, nearly hopping to my car, still beaming from ear to ear.

How could I only celebrate this day, the 16th of September 2022 to the fullest, I ask myself? This present day shall forever be engraved in my history. I excitedly take the rest of the day off work to visit my favourite hairdresser, Alicia. I am bursting, I can barely control myself. On the way to Alicia, I allow myself to let out a huge scream of relief in the car, followed by very loud happy beats that I wholeheartedly sing along to. Swinging while driving to 'Don't stop me now' by Queen, I am feeling the lyrics in my flesh. That particular tune had most certainly become my personal anthem in my rebirth after cancer. It's fearless and filled with forward-pushing energy that barely anyone can resist the temptation of moving along to. I am one lucky girl', I tell myself repeatedly.

I am set on getting long hair extensions. No more, did I want to be reminded of this past cancer hell every time I looked at myself in the mirror. Despite the slow regrowth, I could not bear the sight and texture of the short, thin, fluffy hairdo that Mother Nature forced upon me. Alicia was also the hairdresser, who shaved my head after the first chemotherapy sessions caused my hair to fall out in distressing masses. Back then, my four young children, symbolically, in turns, cut my hair before Alicia grabbed the electric shaver to finish off the imposed Sinéad O'Connor look. Sometimes, I can't believe that this cancer hell really happened. I often allow myself to forget about it, but the lifelong daily invisible handicaps from the treatment quickly remind me that this nightmare was indeed a recent reality.

Tonight, is going to be good. I am going to spoil myself, savour each second of this day and the days to come. I may never really get used to this rollercoaster of emotions post-cancer. The post-traumatic stress disorder (PTSD) associated with cancer is very present despite my outside façade not always reflecting it. Unlike other diseases, cancer seems to be omnipresent. We hear of celebrities losing the battle against cancer on a daily basis. Most people have had a relative affected by cancer and so, it seems the constant reminder is inevitable, no matter how hard one tries to move forward and heal. It feels like whenever I watch a movie or TV show, sooner or later someone gets a cancer diagnosis and more times than not, dramatically dies from the disease.

I can't find the carefree mindset that I had before cancer. No symptom is left unnoticed or ignored. When I have a cough, my mind tells me it's pulmonary metastases. When I have a headache, my mind jumps straight to a diagnosis of brain metastases. When I feel random shoulder or back pain, my mind alerts me I may have bone metastases. Just like people straight away think of Covid-19 once they have a cough, my reflex is biased and it's like I am no longer allowed to experience benign non-cancer related symptoms.

The intense paralysing anxiety before each follow-up and the overwhelming too-good-to-be-true relief after each appointment have somehow become part of my new life. Despite not being able to fully be certain that cancer won't ever show its ugly face again in the future, I remain vigilant and in charge of my own health.

With my chemotherapy port-a-catheter still cosily sitting under my clavicle, I can't fully breathe that sigh of relief just yet. Nevertheless, each good follow-up scan renews my love and respect for this delicious life that I now see very differently than before cancer. Growing old and grey is a privilege. Society conditions us to view ageing as a gloomy prospect that we must face with fear-ridden anticipation. With each year that is added to our lives, we often fall into society's acculturation and adopt the youth-reminiscing depressive attitude. More so when we move up a decade with a new first digit decorating our age.

Many of us never get the chance to climb up the levels and lives are cut short, way too soon. Not everyone is allowed to change their first digit to a 3, 4 or 5 and that is why we must embrace growing older with full gratitude. Counting our blessings to be allowed to continue to participate in this game of life, each day.

It is not a given and we can quickly feel a sense of entitlement, taking it for granted to simply be alive when we do not stop, reflect, and appreciate. Every morning, when I wake up, I pause, and I am consciously grateful to not have died in my sleep. I guess this realisation of our deepest vulnerability is key to a content outlook on life. Nurturing children early on, with this mindset, will undoubtedly reduce the risk of them growing into entitled adults. I try to teach my children to do the right thing, even when nobody is watching. They shall always choose justice over everything else. I can only wish for them to grow up into adults, who will not look away when they see a situation of injustice. I hope I can transfer my ethics onto them, so that they always stand up for the right cause, despite the backlash they may face for going against the flow of an often, greedy, and blind society.

I know it can all be over in a blink of an eye and therefore I, not only try to make the most of it all for myself and my children but I have also learnt many crucial lessons. What is this life worth if you spend it following the masses while not speaking up for what is morally right? What is this life worth if you see social injustice happening before your eyes and you do not dare take a strong stand in contributing, even a tiny percentage to a change in the *status quo*? What I have learnt after cancer is that absolutely nothing is impossible. If I, while receiving the most toxic medical treatment known to mankind, was able to have such a big impact on society by speaking up, I can only imagine how we could all contribute to combatting any social injustice by working together hand in hand, while being physically fit.

The sky is not the limit. I have made it my life mission to advocate for child abuse prevention while empowering others to regard society's labels as superpowers rather than a weakness or failure. Following my poignant TEDx talk in 2021, I started working at my dream job at the Ministry of Education. From the moment I started being transparent in public following the release of my first book, I could finally be my real self without playing a role to quietly fit into society's boxes. I could therefore give my full potential to a topic that was so very close to my heart.

Feeling welcomed and supported by my wonderful work colleagues and employer, I enthusiastically helped setting up a pedagogical project for the prevention of physical, psychological, and sexual abuse of children. The project is aimed at empowering children from a young age for them to be able to set their own body boundaries, recognise good, bad, and strange touch, realise that they are allowed to say no, listen to their intuition, differ between good and bad secrets and encourage them to seek help if required. These principles will be repeatedly taught throughout the years in a positive, gentle, child-friendly manner by integrating theatrical and musical elements.

The project does not focus on the abuse or the abuser *per se* but on the innate resources of the child and its surroundings without putting the sole responsibility on the child to fight the abuser. Giving children the appropriate toolbox from a young age, while gently integrating these basic but crucial principles into their daily lives is the ultimate primary prevention in my eyes. These children will be raised with a correct understanding of what is right and what is wrong and will therefore be given the confidence to seek help more readily than a child who only has the truth of the abuser because of their brainwashing. These children will, one day, become sensitive parents who will naturally pass on these principles to their own children without inhibition, and slowly, the taboo will, drop by drop, disappear from society.

The paradigm shift will eventually happen over time. One small step for these children, one giant leap for mankind. I dream of a world, where children can be children, feel safe and be loved unconditionally. I dream of a world, in which people are treated with kindness and respect. I dream of a world, where we don't need awareness campaigns, awareness days or months in a desperate attempt to eradicate atrocities, that are being enabled by society itself. We all have a small contribution to make each and every day in order to create a better world, for generations to come. We all have a duty of care towards all the children in the world and I can no longer accept inaction in preventing these daily crimes behind closed doors.

The radio is playing the latest hits in the background, while Alicia is attaching the long black hair extensions. Strand by strand, I am going to be sitting in that chair for a few hours. The full head is slowly but surely taking shape and I am happy like a biscuit as we say here in Luxembourg. I am savouring that state of relief, euphoria, and gratitude that I am currently floating in, not wanting this heavenly moment to end. I know that I'll have to come down from my cloud as the days pass by and rationally, I know that the next appointment is waiting for me in three months but until then, I decide to *carpe diem*. Being single for the past nine months, I have thoroughly been enjoying the freedom that comes with not making compromises.

All around us, every individual is a hidden treasure. Each one of us carries a life story in his or her backpack but we often don't dare to discover others. We still abide by the 'don't talk to strangers' order that we have fully integrated since childhood. We fear the stranger on the bus, we avoid eye contact and get uncomfortable if they smile at us. I often make bets with myself. I smile at a stranger and see if he or she smiles back. Not a creepy smile, just a kind, gentle smile. Most of the time, the smile doesn't get returned to the sender, often misinterpreted as either flirting or mocking.

We are not used to these random human connections anymore. I imagine that it must have been easier back in the time when phones did not steal that last remaining opportunity for everyday affinities between individuals. I also believe that mobile phones, growing into an extension of the human limb, have caused people to become less empathetic towards each other. Qualities like kindness and empathy need training and if we do not give these attributes space in everyday life, we become colder towards each other. Disconnected from reality, we will not see the opportunities to help others with an act of kindness. Be it at the park, at work, on the bus, every day, people would be grateful for a hand. As a community, we do not have the reflex anymore to just help without asking anything in return. Our society has become very individualistic and children, mirroring what they see every day, they will be more interested in themselves than the community as a whole. Teaching empathy and kindness must start very early on, at home and at school; this should constitute a major part in the upbringing of a child.

Why have we become so complicated? Speaking to strangers every day is the ultimate beauty of life. Regardless of social status, educational background, race, religion, age, gender, and every other element that makes up who we are. We all walk through life with a puzzle, our world vision. We have our convictions and principles that are quite firm and may not budge. Then, we have our understanding of the world we live in that can only be changed by reading, discussing, and debating. Unless we speak to people we don't know, our puzzle will forever remain the same. In order to grow, we need to give that puzzle the chance to be completed or modulated and the only way to do that is by exchanging life stories. If we always hang out with the same circle of friends, we will not be able to grow efficiently. We know our friends' puzzles, they know ours and so, there won't be any substantial added value.

Despite being mostly alone, I am in no way lonely. Many people get uncomfortable, even scared to remain alone with their thoughts. I thoroughly enjoy conversations with strangers on a daily basis. It's like an unquenchable thirst that I have which helps me discover the meaning of life. I can only recommend speaking to strangers, regardless of who they are. Even conversing with a right-wing extremist for example is essential. It is interesting for me to understand how a person deviates to this point. I find the French expression 'Il faut de tout pour faire un monde' very important when looking at the world. We need the sweet and the bitter people. We can't only have the sweet side of the world as it would not challenge us to change for the better. We need the bitter side, to be able to question the *status quo* and push for change and growth. There has never been a revolution without resistance. The bitter people will always be there, so we might as well use them as a drive to leave behind a better world for our children.

After cancer, I quickly realised that the relationships I had built over time with men and women were not of the healthiest type. I concluded that I may not have been aware of the innumerable red flags because I did not feel love or respect for myself back then. That lack of self-worth, therefore, attracted men and women, who felt the need to play the 'saviour' role in my misery, and misery I had plenty of. Strangely, it was at my absolute worst shape during chemotherapy, hairless and aesthetically not conforming to society's beauty standards, that I finally reconciled myself with my own body.

That broken relationship that was incited by the cruelties of my abuser over decades, had to be restored in order for me to finally realise my own self-value and consequently unconditionally love myself. I even wrote a love letter to my body, which can be found at the back of this book. Once I did that, I evidently set the bar high and therefore the base for a friendship or relationship would undoubtedly be healthier from then on. Both parties would need to be financially, emotionally, and physically stable at the start of the relationship so that neither would need to find a utility in the other person's suffering. That healthy friendship or relationship would therefore better withstand life's adversities than if there was a stability gap between both people from the beginning.

Naturally, by finally loving myself, I now tend to attract the right match of people while sniffing out the potentially incompatible ones more readily. That realisation was key in filtering out the toxic relationships from my life following cancer.

It had been four years since the infamous discovery of Felix's extensive adultery throughout our ten-year marriage. Four years since Felix remorselessly caused a tsunami in our idyllic family life when I was heavily pregnant with our fifth baby. With that discovery, a whirlwind of an unimaginable cascade effect pursued with all its faces, the good, the bad, and the ugly.

Staying true to himself, Felix shamelessly summoned me to court while I was in the middle of a horrendous chemotherapy. As one can imagine, I was physically and emotionally broken during that time, involuntarily rocking the bald look. I could not believe how that man could scrape some more audacity with the most controversial lawyer by his side in order to start a custody battle with the mother of his five children while she was fighting an aggressive form of cancer and fearing for her life.

I was gobsmacked to say the least and could not understand how and why nobody was stopping him. Where were his parents, his brothers, his aunts, his sisters-in-law to tell him that this move was totally misplaced? Or worse, who was perhaps encouraging him to metaphorically kick the mother of his children in the face, while she was already knocked out on the floor from the nasty cancer treatment? What went wrong in this man's upbringing? What surprised me the most, however, is the sole justification from Felix and his lawyer on which basis they thought it would be a brilliant idea to start the custody battle: my cancer. It was suddenly a golden opportunity, it seemed. Thankfully, the justice system in Luxembourg showed some decency and refused to accept Felix's request, kindly reminding him that it was inappropriate and that he should wait until his ex-wife was physically human again to be fighting her at the tribunal.

Many months later, I should have been slowly regaining my physical and emotional strength but instead, found myself back in the courtroom next to Felix. Depleting my residual energy, emotions, and finances, I spent the months of convalescence after the horrors of cancer, worrying about the welfare of our children. As Felix and his lawyer felt that they were navigating on the losing end during the court hearing, his lawyer pulled out the good old *VICTIM* card. How could Felix believe that this was still some sort of a joker?

It's like that victim tag on my forehead was there to stay forever and ever. It's like no matter, how much I repeatedly proved myself to be a survivor, many people would still ruthlessly take advantage of that label to try and build a story around it in their favour. In this case, sitting in the courtroom, Felix and his lawyer started fabling that because I had a 'heavy past', I apparently had considerable trauma, which supposedly meant that I have a pathological obsession with my children and therefore needed some time alone without them so that I could undergo therapy to fix myself.

That 'heavy past' argument was also used by Felix when I found out about his chronic adultery during our marriage. It was his sole justification for cheating on me, blaming me yet again for his own wrongdoings. I could not believe that these two people sitting next to me were actually uttering these words. I could not believe that Felix could go this low after having caused me so much grief already. One thing I knew for sure was that this lack of empathy, the sense of entitlement, the compulsive lying, and the violence were not the ethics that I wanted our children to be predominantly absorbing while they were growing into decent members of our society.

Facing my death, I embarked on a self-discovery journey and strangely, things suddenly start to make sense when one has a more objective view on them. Asking myself the question repeatedly, I could not understand how I ended up marrying Felix, who, in hindsight, is so very incompatible with me, especially when it comes to moral values. I quickly realised that I only repeated the same pattern that I had known all my life from home and that I was familiar with. People often choose a life partner that resembles their dominant parent. Enduring horrors since childhood, I grew up with no self-confidence, hugely lacking self-love and became an avid people-pleaser. The perfect prey for a narcissistic pervert, all over again.

A wolf in sheep's clothing, Felix slowly began to reveal his true self over the years. Men and women presenting with this personality disorder will often be attracted to empaths and vice versa. Since narcissists rely on exclusive attention, an empathetic person would naturally be the perfect fit. Narcissists have insecurity issues, often have a negative self-image, and therefore lie, manipulate, and belittle others to boost their own self-esteem. One big characteristic they all share is that they lack empathy and are unable to recognise the needs of others. They mostly play the 'victim' role in any conflict even if they are blatantly the perpetrator. They have an impressive talent for guilt-tripping others, which is basically emotional manipulation through which they try to get their way like a spoilt child throwing a tantrum on a supermarket floor.

Immersed in the chit-chat with Alicia, I don't look at my phone for a few hours when suddenly I get a call from an unknown number. I wonder who that could be as it's not the familiar number from school, so it can't be an issue with any of my children. Therefore, nothing in the world could be important enough for me to pick up that phone. Nevertheless, I momentarily descend from my happy cloud to answer it. It's the probation officer who has been following my abuser after his release from prison. What could be so important for him to call about, I wonder. With a calm and apologetic voice, he announces that my mother has passed away in the UK. I don't seem to fully grasp the news but acknowledge the information given before telling him that I'll pass by later that day. He also gives me a phone number to call in case I wished to speak to the bereavement officer at the hospital.

From one euphoric moment to the absolute opposite, I am unsure how to feel about this incoming brutal news. I am sensing a mixture of sadness, confusion, anger, and relief, all at once. I am shocked about the synchronicity of it all and my mind is racing with questions. How could my mother and myself both receive a cancer diagnosis at the same time? How could both our ordeals start at the same time with the same abuser? How did she die? Was she alone? Was she in pain? How on Earth was she refused cancer treatment by her family, mostly working in the medical field? How did she feel about her second-born child for the past 30 years? Did she ever love me like she loved her other five children? Can I gather enough courage to call that number given and possibly fly to the UK for a last goodbye?

Shell-shocked by this news, I naturally go into my familiar dissociation survival mode. I still have a couple of hours in that chair at the hairdresser and I let Alicia know what the phone call was about. It's as if saying these words out loud makes it all real. In my rational mind, my mother's death was a logical inevitable consequence of cancer freely evolving without any medical interference whatsoever. Nevertheless, I can't help but feel very angry with the six family members who willingly let her die. That death could have easily been avoided had she been surrounded by people who actually cared about her. She never deserved that life of pain.

The few hours after that call taste bittersweet. The euphoria from earlier was definitely damped and overshadowed by the sad news of my mother's passing. Strangely, a few weeks earlier, I had been suffering from a bout of horrible insomnia, which I could not figure out the cause of. Perhaps, my mother's impending demise was keeping me awake at night?

Could we really have been connected in that manner? I am suddenly feeling a huge sense of survivor's guilt, which persists for the rest of the day.

On the way back to my car and with tears in my eyes, I dial the number of the morgue. A kind voice picks up and asks me who I am. After being presented with heartfelt condolences, I ask about the cause of death, and the lady answers 'metastatic breast cancer'. The lady continues by asking whether I would like to stop by, which I kindly decline as this was too close to home after facing my own death not too long ago. I just can't be confronted with that particular topic anytime soon as I also nearly ended up in a morgue. It was simply too fresh for me, and I also avoid going to funerals in general. The psychological wound of cancer was by far not healed and so staying away from anything death-related was the appropriate self-protection for me at this time.

The tears continued flowing in the car. Was the death of my mother a painful reminder of what I had missed with the absence of a mother in my life? The day was not supposed to end like this. This day was meant to be a good one, it had started so well after all with the happy news of a clear scan.

There was no way I could find an ounce of desire deep down to celebrate the news of my cancer being in remission. It felt absolutely wrong if I even dared to enjoy the day any further. I had to write, that's my only way of liberating whatever was accumulating inside and that I could not verbally put into words. Writing was not only my therapy but also a powerful vector that I could use to give others a voice; those who can relate to the same feelings of despair but also of strength and determination.

While I also use writing as a weapon, many people assume that this is driven by revenge but that is not the case. Exposing moral injustice and its perpetrators sends a clear message to current or potential abusers in that their deeds will not remain in silence or behind closed doors where they occur in the first place. Through my work, I am warning all these people enjoying criminal immunity. By creating a victim, they are essentially indirectly feeding into his or her superpower that may be invisible at the time of the crime, but will ultimately return to catch up with them, even many decades later.

Sitting at home that evening, I decided to write a letter to my mother even though she will never read these words. I could not start my letter with 'Dear Mama, mum, mother' or any other variant for that matter. This was impossible after the disconnection I have felt with her over the years and the deep feeling of betrayal I had accumulated.

I knew that I had to let time pass and feel what I had to feel without a filter. Following the publication of that letter, Andreas wrote me a message, telling me that I was the sole reason why our mother was sick and that I would go to hell. I kindly replied that I had already been through several hells and that perhaps, it was now somebody else's turn.

Dear Nora,

Today, I received the news of your death.

Strangely, it coincided with the same day I received the sweetest news that I am allowed to live on...

I knew this day was approaching, rather sooner than later, while we were both fighting cancer, only you were not allowed to fight at all...

Perhaps my sleepless nights sensed your impending demise. I would like to believe that we were at least connected in that way.

I am unsure of my emotions after today's news...is it sadness? anger? relief? empathy? pity? confusion?

Perhaps, it is a mix of all of them. Will I go through the grieving process as a daughter would? Only time will tell...

Truth is, in my books, you already died a long time ago, along with the rest of this family.

I will never know if you have ever loved me like you loved your other 5 children.

I have no happy memories to fall back on. Very early

on, I felt your rejection and have always tried to excuse it, but that was too easy.

My recent post about cancer choosing the most kind-hearted people is very timely because you were a very kind woman even if that kindness was never directed towards me...you never deserved a life full of misery.

You failed to protect me from the obvious hell I was trapped in, fully at the mercy of your devil husband. I forgive you for that.

When that monster was officially convicted for hurting your little girl for all these years, you still stood by him and you asked me to go to church to confess what I did to him. I forgive you for that.

We both received our cancer diagnosis at the same time, only you, despite being a competent doctor, were denied surgery, chemo, and radiotherapy by the people who were meant to care for you.

You were fully at the mercy of that devil and none of your 5 children, namely Andreas, Denise, Leonard, Elena, and Mira bothered to insist that you receive any cancer treatment at all.

I will never know how it feels to have a mother (or parent at all) who cares about me and loves me unconditionally like I am able to with my own children.

I can't lose something I never had in the first place.

I can't miss something I never had the chance to experience.

...and so even though I so wished that your devil husband would have been the one in that morgue today, I am sorry that you were the one to go first.

Rest in peace, Nora, I finally forgive you.

Mary

Dubai, 1983

Chapter Two

The Quest

Over the next few days, I felt very guilty for being safe (for now) from cancer while my mother was not lucky enough to make it. Whenever I was sad about my mother's death, I felt wrong to feel that way. It was as if I was not allowed to be upset as I never had the chance to experience the mother-daughter relationship that many girls seemed to have. It nearly felt like I was an imposter. That emotion had been very familiar to me since being a child. With each life achievement, I could never appreciate it like other people in my surrounding would.

I viewed myself as a fraud and that one day I was going to be exposed, despite rationally knowing that I worked hard and deserved full merit. Imposter syndrome is a very common occurrence for people who experienced childhood trauma. Feelings of intense self-doubt that persevere despite education, experience, and accomplishments will cause the person to work harder and put higher expectations on themselves, constantly feeling that they are not 'good enough'. To not make my children assume that they upset me, I explained to them that my mother had died and that is why I may be a little sad these days.

They started asking more and more questions about their grandmother, whom they had never met. Up until then, I avoided talking about her but had definitely put her in the 'bad people' category for my children. That way, they would never sense the need to go look for my side of the family. I transmitted the bad image that I had of my mother to my children by saying that she had not protected me from the devil father and that she was not worthy of being called 'family'. I was fully convinced that I had no good memories to fall back on when it came to her. I fully believed the narrative that I grew up with; that my mother was crazy, that she hated me and that she failed to protect me while standing by the side of my abuser during the criminal trial and following his release from prison.

Feelings of anger were starting to bubble up. Anger towards my former family who shamelessly let her die in terrible pain over two years. I could not understand how this could have happened. I could not get rid of that nagging need to understand the full puzzle of my past. I grew up with many gaps that I was unable to make sense of because I was too young at the time. It's like the death of my mother triggered this overwhelming desire to understand what exactly happened back in the 90s, but also what exactly had happened in the past two years. I felt pushed to get my mother justice and make the people accountable for failing to protect her. For me, the sense of justice prevailed despite not being fully at peace with her. Despite all the past failings, I could forgive her because I knew that she had spent the last thirty years under heavy anti-psychotic drugs in an awful inhumane passive physical and mental state.

I began thinking about how I could find the answers I desperately required to complete my puzzle. Who could I talk to? I remembered the name of the psychiatrist who treated my mother back then, and I called him after all these years. I had to meet him and potentially ask him all the questions that remained unanswered over three decades. I did not know whether he was still working but I tried my luck and low and behold, I managed to organise a meeting with him a couple of weeks later.

Meanwhile, I thought hard about all the hospitals that my mother had visited in Luxembourg and abroad. I then created an investigative drawing board on which I would put all my thoughts and link them as detectives do in movies. I was pushed by an intense drive to get answers. I had no idea what exactly I was looking for, but my intuition drove me to contact all these hospitals in order to receive my mother's medical archives from the past decades. I am very connected to my intuition and often just follow it without rationally questioning it. I may not always know why that strong push is there, but I just do what I feel I must do, and later on it all usually makes sense. It's as if that gut feeling was stronger than me and I could not resist it.

My intuition has saved my life over and over again. It has always been my loyal company. I did not have anything healthy to rely on when I was a child. Growing up in an utterly perverted system, there was no physical reference person to guide me. Therefore, the relationship with my intuition is very intense as I've been strengthening it since childhood, and it has been in constant activation with the chronic exposure to danger. It had been two weeks since asking for the medical files. It was not a given that anyone could receive these records, regardless of the link to the deceased patient. Every day after work, with a pounding heart, I impatiently checked my letterbox to see whether any of the hospitals had sent anything.

It was a Thursday afternoon when the first letter with a CD safely arrived in my hands. Thursday has always been my lucky weekday. I always counted on Thursdays to bring me good news. The address of origin on the envelope reads the psychiatric hospital in Ettelbruck, which is the largest facility in Luxembourg. Generally, as children, we grew up with the understanding that *Ettelbruck* was a synonym for the location where the lunatic population of the country was held in white straitjackets under lock and key. I was very familiar with that building. It was tall, grey, and cold. It was very unwelcoming. I still remember the aura of the inside of that hospital.

We used to go there to visit our mother when we were children. It would be an excursion type trip overshadowed with anxious anticipation during the long car journey. The hospital was next to a football pitch and that's where I used to play with my siblings when our mother was allowed to have her one-hour-break in the fresh air before returning to her 'prison'. My mother would be so excited; like a child allowed to go outside to play in the garden. Back inside, it was always a struggle for her to realise that she had to stay and not be allowed to return home with her children, on the sole insistence of her husband.

As children, we mostly saw mentally ill people sitting in rooms staring into the emptiness. Others were busy with creative activities like painting or knitting. I never liked going there as a child. It was always very intimidating. The psychiatrist and the nurses would question us. We would see our mother imprisoned, unknowingly initiated by the statements that our father made us repeat. Opening the envelope, I had no idea what I was about to discover. To make things more suspenseful, I had no way of reading a CD with my laptop.

Modern laptops are just too flat. CDs seemed to be an ancient artefact as I had a hard time finding a CD drive to open the files. After several searches, the moment had come to finally read that CD. The loading of 30 years of cruelty seemed to be taking an eternity. My heart was beating at full speed. I was very nervous. I had even scratched my car mirror while parking earlier as I just couldn't wait to check the letter box. It was a Thursday after all, so I was extra optimistic.

While the CD was loading, my mind was travelling back and forth. I vividly pictured the recurrent police interventions when I was just a child in the 1990s. I remembered how each trip to the psychiatric hospital followed the same pattern. My mother would do something that angered her husband, yet again. This could be mixing different food ingredients that were not up to his taste. She could have mixed the wrong-coloured garments in the washing machine. She could have cooked too much food. She could have used the wrong product to clean the sink. He would get utterly mad and openly hit her in front of their children.

He used to hurt her with his bare hands or used any item that he could grab within his reach. Most of the time, his weapon consisted of a heavy bundle of what seemed like a million keys that he walked around with. One could always hear that monster coming from afar, just by the sound of these keys jangling. My mother would cry out in pain and sadly had nobody on her side to help her. She would never give him the upper hand, despite him being physically stronger than her. After shamelessly hurting and humiliating her in front of their six children, he would command all of them to go upstairs.

I had to take my younger siblings with me as ordered as they were very young at the time, Mira was only one year old when our mother was first brutally removed from the family home. Nicolas would then threaten his wife that he would call the police and ambulance to collect her. We were upstairs, terrified of the violence occurring downstairs. We could hear how our mother, who was already on the floor at that point and tied with ropes to the radiator, was pleading with her husband not to call the police and not to give her *Haldol*. She was used to getting regular injections of this potent neuroleptic drug, so that she would forcibly be kept quiet.

Nicolas never felt any empathy or pity for the mother of his six children, who would be on the ground, showing the white flag, crying in pain and fear. He was a savage. I would hear him call the regular family doctor Dr. M., the police, and the ambulance. Often, when he had his hands full, torturing his wife, he would order us children to call Dr M., the police, and the ambulance. It always felt as if these three parties arrived at the given address at light-speed.

Before my mother could flee the house or evoke any sort of physical resistance, two policemen would make sure that she had no chance of moving any limb. They often came in pairs. The sight of policemen in uniform repeatedly at our home was very frightening for us. They would hold our mother with brutal force as if they were restraining a heavy criminal. I remember how my mother once pulled the ear of a bald police officer in self-defence before he got livid and slammed her with full force on the bumper of the police car.

To make things worse, this scene happened in front of the family house in full sight allowing the neighbours to watch the spectacle. After being fully restrained by the police in complete public humiliation, Dr. M.

would take his loaded syringe out of his bag and inject the powerful anti-psychotic drug into our mother's thigh, just like you would shoot a huge elephant to the ground with an anaesthetic. She had no chance.

With the drug slowly absorbing into her system, my mother became more and more passive and so the paramedics had an easier time escorting her to the ambulance. They would then transport her to the psychiatric hospital in the north of the country for another long stay away from her children. The CD finished loading. I then open, what seems, like endless scanned files. What a tedious task for the hospital to dig out these archives from the 90s, that were probably sitting in the basement, collecting dust. I was very grateful to obtain them.

I am trembling with fear, horror, sadness, relief, curiosity, and excitement all at once. Was I finally going to be able to complete my puzzle that had massive gaps over the past decades? I scrolled through hundreds of pages filled with medical reports, labs, scans, diaries, requests, approvals, interviews, and handwritten and typed letters from the abuser himself, surprisingly also signed by us as children. I honestly didn't know where to start.

The first document that struck my sight was a medical report, which was written a few years before I pressed charges for child sexual abuse against my father. Looking through the files, I quickly realise that these archives contained so many precious elements that could have accelerated the criminal investigations back then and confirmed the truth sooner than it did. What a shame that the investigators never got hold of these hundreds of pages. In that particular document, it is mentioned that my mother who worked as a gynaecologist obstetrician abroad before settling down in Luxembourg is fully dependent on her husband with whom she has six children. It says that she is submissive to him and very devoted to her children.

The report pursues in describing her as dignified, highly educated, and very cultivated, however, her life is that of a woman who is erased, with no ambition or interest. The psychiatrist writing the report then wonders how is it that this woman, despite her acquired wealth (cultural, professional, and social), despite the enthusiasm and that little spark of joy that she manifests sometimes, remains a woman who is not the actress of her own life? Is it cultural? Is she pretending? Has she just given up? Is it due to an actual psychiatric condition? For now, the psychiatrist concludes, it is very difficult to know more about this woman, as long as the SECRETS in this family are kept under lock and key.

Reading that sentence broke my heart into a billion pieces and I started trembling. That report is talking about family secrets just a few years before my abuser got arrested. How could that report be missed? Could it be that my mother was not crazy and that she tried to protect me all these years? Could it be that I did not fully understand her involvement during the sixteen-year-long hell that I went through at the hands of that monster? I finished reading the report which stated that Nicolas imposed the law of silence on his whole surrounding.

The psychiatrist wonders whether one should consider that there may be an extreme case of abuse by this man towards his wife in order to understand the real situation of this patient. Then, he cites a few examples to underline his suspicion. Nicolas installed digital door locks on doors inside and outside of the house, for which only he and his children knew the code. Nicolas forbids his wife to cook in her own kitchen, so the meals are always ready prepared such as frozen pizzas.

The report continues to describe Nicolas as the sole decision-maker in the house and that his wife has no voice. It also says that he has brought a young woman to live with them, despite the opposition of his wife. The final sentence of that report concludes that this woman was exhausted of resistance against her husband to the point of being hospitalised by him time and time again. Little did I know that this statement was just the first of hundreds of horror stories that I had not known about until getting hold of that folder. With each page that I read, the sadness about the hell that my mother went through intensified.

It was as if I was getting to know the mother that I never had. Many were diaries that nurses wrote to document her days at the closed psychiatric facility. These pages were precious in every sense of the word. They embedded so much suffering that I started to question everything. There were reports of broken ribs, physical violence by her husband, and even mentions of Nicolas SEXUALLY ABUSING children. This last statement was written in the context of an interview with my mother's brother. During the criminal investigations, this 'detail' could have been a game changer.

My uncle has not been invited once to the police station to testify during the investigations and of course, he himself didn't offer to give his two cents either. He could have shared this information and even more: all accomplices. This uncle used to come to our home to watch porn with his dear brother-in-law. The two of them were always casually speaking with me about sex, despite me being very underage. The fact that a child was very uncomfortable seemed to be amusing to these two men.

We, as a society, all failed my mother. Even her children grew up to side with the father and to principally be 'against' the mother as she was to be regarded as 'crazy'. We patronised her, and gave no credit to whatever, she would voice. She had lost her dignity a long time ago and that medical folder was just clear proof that these crimes were committed by Nicolas.

As the days passed, my love and empathy for my mother grew stronger and I was finally struck by the grief I thought I would not be able to feel after my mother passed away. I was filled with immense guilt of not having been able to rescue her. I felt upset that my children never had the opportunity to meet their grandmother. I could not get over the fact that the image of my mother was falsified by my abuser.

I felt the strong need to get her justice and reinstate her dignity, even more after reading through the pages that depict a broken woman. How could both our nightmares have started in 1992? Was there a crucial piece of the puzzle that I was missing all these years? It can't have been a coincidence, can it? What if my mother never resented me as I thought she did for all these years? As recorded, it turned out that she attempted to kill my father on many occasions using a knife or hammer. I was quite pleased to read that. Could it be that she tried to kill the man that she knew was sexually abusing her eldest daughter? Pushed by this intense sense of justice, I unconsciously started writing this current book.

It was of the highest importance that the truth shall not be buried with my mother; just like I wrote my first book out of fear that my truth would be buried if I had not survived cancer. These cruelties needed to be exposed. Black on white without filter, for my mother, for me, for my children, and for generations to come. Strangely, as the days went by since first reading through these pages, it seemed that the memory drawers that were tightly shut in my mind were starting to burst open. It's as if the good memories that I actually did have of my mother were resurfacing after my puzzle was slowly being completed.

Mental images of my childhood started to reappear, the good, the bad, and the ugly. This time, armed with the truth in those documents, I could have an objective view of these memories. This time, they would not be skewed by the brainwashing from my abuser.

Making butter and jam sandwiches for my children one morning, I suddenly said to them 'my mother also used to make me jam and butter sandwiches when I was little'. This may seem like a simple sentence to most, but it bore a very strong underlying meaning considering the loathe I grew up with. This sentence became the first of many to follow, with which the ultimate reconciliation with my deceased mother would commence. I started telling my children how my mother used to make me carrots with mayonnaise, peel and cut apples for me, and prepare my favourite salad with tomatoes and cumin.

She used to make me black tea with milk and bring it to me. She used to tell me that she put a lot of milk to protect the lining of my stomach from the tea. I told my children that she was the one who pierced my ears when I was little. I remembered how I loved being close to her, that she smelled nice, and that I was always trying to get her attention while doing my best to remain as far as possible from my abuser. I remember that she used to go to bed very early because she would take strong sleeping pills. She would cover herself in a thick layer of *Nivea* cream from head to toe. Perhaps her way of keeping her abuser away from her at night? Nicolas would always comment on how he found that cream repugnant and that he couldn't kiss her because of it.

My mother loved cooking and there was absolutely nothing wrong with it. Had I had contact with her over the past years, I would not have feared my mother cooking for my children. I remember regularly waking up to a delicious smell in the house, which would drive my father mad, and he would get her brutally hospitalised for it. It is horrifying when one thinks about it. To be violently removed from your family home, away from your children, baby included, just because you cooked. Your husband, who is not happy with its taste, then fabricates a whole story around your cooking, convincing doctors that your cooking was excessive and your ingredients incompatible, hence you must be crazy. This is followed by violence, pain, and humiliation.

As a grand finale, the episode proceeds with police, injections, an ambulance, and another long stay in a psychiatric hospital with real patients who are on the psychiatry ward for the right reasons. How could this have happened time and again without child protection services getting involved? How was it possible that nobody stopped this man? Repressed happy memories included me travelling alone by bus with my mother to Luxembourg city to buy clothes. I used to feel privileged to be the one out of six children to be allowed to go with her and enjoyed the one to one with her. All this, of course, was before she was put on the many dreadful medications. Back then, she was still full of life, her face had colour and she was reactive. I told my children how my mother was always gentle, smart, soft-spoken, never shouted at her children, and was always smiley when she was not being tortured by her husband.

Saying that out loud, I realised that these are traits that I most certainly inherited from her. In that sense, I confirm that when my abuser used to say that I was like my mother (during his defence in court, stating that I was schizophrenic like her), he was without a doubt right, but not in the way, he intended it to be. Indeed, I inherited the beauty, intelligence, and strength from her and nothing at all from him, thank God. I knew that my gentle parenting with my own children was the result of the kind parenting I witnessed as a child despite the hell I was going through in parallel. The mind is powerful.

In order to survive unimaginable situations, the victim will dissociate body and mind to not be able to feel the intensity of the pain in real time. These memories can be stored in a compartment for decades, until a triggering event, such as death, will make that drawer burst open. In this case, the happy memories had also been stored away based on the associated brainwashing that my abuser had performed since childhood and have only now finally reappeared. Memories of my mother cutting my nails appeared and how it hurt as she would cut them too short. This may seem insignificant to many but implies that my mother cared for me and did not neglect me as I had it anchored in my mind all these years.

Slowly the puzzle pieces were coming together. Another memory popped up from our time in Remich. As children, Leonard stabbed me with a pen in my head. The apparent reason was that I scribbled on his magazine after he drew on my homework. Fair enough. Shocked about her son's brutality, my mother put ground coffee on my head to stop the bleeding, which surprisingly worked. This specific episode became the running joke over the following decades and her husband would use it as another reason to pretend his wife was 'crazy'. Many years later, I realised that using ground coffee to stop bleeding from a small cut is evidence-based and there was nothing 'crazy' about it. Quite the contrary, as it was a rather smart idea from my mother.

I felt a strong desire to repair the false image that I had transmitted to my children before I got hold of the truth. I could not tolerate the thought of my children growing up with a wrong reality as my genitor had done with me and my siblings. Even as a child, I was immensely empathetic. I have always had this overwhelming sense of justice, often for people being discriminated against. As a child, I could not bear or tolerate other children ganging up against another child to mock him or her. Perhaps, because, I was also bullied daily by my own siblings? I could relate to the feelings of the isolated victim. I could never truly believe what my father was telling us about our mother. I felt very sad for what my mother was going through. I used to hide and watch in disbelief how my father would repeatedly hurt her. I was convinced that my mother was not sick but merely sad.

As a child, I quickly understood that my mother was not happy. She wanted to get a divorce after Mira was born. I knew that she loved her children but didn't necessarily want that many. She had other aspirations than being a wife and mother of six children. I was alone in my hell and so was my mother. How I wished I had been able to join forces with her and fight the devil together. We both had the same abuser, but it was very obvious, however, that I neither had the maturity nor the necessary perspective to bring him down. I was in the obsessive possession of my abuser for over 16 years and there was absolutely no way out. My mother remained in that hell for over 30 years until her final days.

I started speaking to nurses who had cared for my mother over the years. I needed to have as many details as possible about her. It was like I needed to reconstruct the narrative in my mind, but this time, my mother would be in the 'good' camp. I was convinced that she did not belong on the blacklist like the other members of my family who betrayed me. Armed with documents that would constitute the absolute evidence for the new narrative, I didn't have a single doubt in my mind that my mother loved me.

The nurses I spoke to could remember her as gentle, smart, and kind. They, of course, also remember her as being defiant when they came home to inject her every month against her will with a potent drug, that in hindsight was totally unnecessary. It was the perfect pretext for the abuser to oppress his wife, who may get in the way of his perverted actions on his daughter.

I have often thought that my mother did not possess the inner strength and resilience that I do. I understood, however, that I would not have been able to fight the way I do today, had I also been perpetually silenced physically and mentally with powerful drugs. My mother had no chance of scraping some more energy to resist. She was alone against her husband, her children, the police as well as the medical team. She was always going to draw the shortest straw, no matter what. My abuser often threatened to send me to the same psychiatric hospital as he used to do to his wife. I was smart enough to understand that this would be my destiny if I didn't conform as expected of me. It would have been so easy for him to lock me up for the rest of my life in that hospital. I grew up with a great fear of that place, as if it was a haunted house.

The other patients, who were rightfully there would be staring at these six children visiting their mother. I was already creeped out by only being in that location for a short visit. I could not imagine how my mother must have felt being stuck in there against her will, on continuous tranquillisers and surrounded by heavily psychotic patients. Scrolling through the pages, the abuse my mother endured only seemed to worsen over the years. I had to stop reading at some point as it became too overwhelming for me to handle. With the ability to vividly visualise the scenes that I was reading, it really felt as if I was experiencing the pain of my mother at the time.

It's as if I was living these episodes through the pages. I avoided going through the diaries in the evenings as I would be haunted with lively images once I closed my eyes at night. On the one hand, I was petrified to read about the atrocities that my dear mother was subjected to, but on the other hand, it was pleasant to read the positive input from the doctors and nurses about her. The description of her daily activities and her personality when she was off the medication gave me new happy memories to add to my drawer that had been tightly shut over the past three decades.

Away from her aggressor, my mother could thrive, she could be herself for a little while without being tormented by him and that was so nice for me to read. When she was not in her 'prison', she loved joining elderly people on bus tours to Germany. She also used to travel alone on fully organised trips to Spain. She would come back filled with life, only to be put back on the zombie-inducing drugs. What was her favourite colour? Did she have hobbies? What was her favourite food? What kind of music did she like? I did not really know my mother as I was too focused on surviving and escaping my father, that I never had the opportunity to truly connect with her.

The justice system in Luxembourg most surely failed in that they released this criminal from prison early. Perhaps, I would have found the courage to reconnect with my mother after the trial, had this criminal not been in the picture. He was always going to be around and after sending him to prison, there was no way, I could risk confrontation with this devil.

I rather distanced myself from my whole toxic family while building my own little family. How I now wished this evil man had been kept behind bars and I could have introduced my mother to my children. I could have rescued her from this family. I could have got her off these drugs and made her blossom into a human being again after that man consistently worked on stealing her spark throughout the years. Writing these lines, I am saddened to my core. I felt powerless. My children would have given her joy, I am certain. Children have that power. They would have warmed her heart again after it had gone ice-cold from decades of torture. She would have regained colour in her face after the heavy medications she was unnecessarily on for decades, sucked all life out of her. She was dead and alive at the same time. I deeply regret to not have been holding this crucial, game-changing medical folder sooner.

To slightly relieve that guilt, I took my children to the cemetery where their sister is buried, and the four children let balloons fly up high as a symbolic goodbye. It was very important for me that my children would grow up with a positive image of my mother. It was the least I could do now to redeem myself for not being courageous enough to see through the lies and the brainwashing that my abuser perfectly put in place to get his way, time and time again. My mother's legacy will live on with my children through this current book and the few happy memories that have resurfaced since her death.

The day had come to meet the psychiatrist, who treated my mother back in the 90's. I was a child when I saw him last. He hadn't changed much. Apart from the grey hair, he was still the calm, kind, smiley man that I remembered him as. I offered him my book as a gift. It was necessary for me to give him the family context, so that he would be able to understand the full picture. During the conversation, the question was raised whether my mother became sick because she saw what was happening to her daughter or had she been pretending to be sick to drive my abuser to the edge? Was that her way of protecting me while being on heavy anti-psychotics? My heart dropped. At that moment, everything made sense.

Many questions may forever remain unanswered but the fact that both our ordeals started in 1992 can't be a coincidence. I was clinging onto the theory that regardless of the diagnosis, the medical folder definitely proved to me that my mother loved me and tried to protect me from my abuser as well as she could. That was factual. I have heard, on several occasions, a parent stating that they would kill their partner if they found out that they were sexually abusing their child, even with gory details of how they would do it, which mostly included castrating the abuser in one way or the other.

The attempted murders as documented in the folder, further confirmed that she tried to protect me from her abusive husband. What a pity that she never succeeded. She would have freed me from my hell while I would have pleaded with the judge not to punish my mother as it was necessary to get rid of this sadist, for the greater good.

There was no added value in keeping that monster in society. In the USA, child molesters get 100 years and more of prison and/or get executed. I wished sentences in Luxembourg would have been similar in this regard. That would have spared so much suffering over the past decades and my mother would most definitely be alive today.

One by one, the medical files have been arriving between my hands. A total of seven hospitals in Luxembourg and beyond. Reading through over three thousand pages, I was able to get a snapshot of this sad, destroyed life perpetrated by the actions of one single criminal. These pages were proof of how only one person was able to manipulate his surroundings and go to extreme lengths to break a gentle soul. How could this man be let loose in society to continue hurting the people that depended on him, or more rightly, who he conditioned to believe that they depended on him?

At first sight, what this man did to my mother may seem like an aggravated case of Munchausen syndrome by proxy, which is a psychological disorder marked by attention-seeking behaviour by a caregiver through those who are in their care. They often make up symptoms or cause symptoms by deliberate actions. Healthcare providers often have a hard time identifying the cause of the symptoms and therefore also have difficulties recognising that the symptoms are caused by the caregiver. This explanation, however, would be too easy.

This would relinquish my genitor from taking responsibility for his actions by blaming a psychological condition. He's been psychologically assessed on several occasions and is mentally very sound and therefore knows exactly what he's doing. He made sure that my mother remained sick, and he has always embraced the role of the caring husband and father that has sacrificed everything for his six children despite his wife's illness. He ensured that my mother becomes fully dependent on him.

He used to do that with all his children. Through his psychological abuse, he would make his wife and children dependent on him and they would truly believe that they could not survive without him. He knew what he was doing, and the following pages of this book will enlighten the reader by taking this man apart, step by step or in other words, dissecting him.

Over the following days, a particular song struck

my attention as it was so fitting to what I was going through. This song became my anthem for my investigation, the quest of finding out what exactly happened to my mother. I could not stop playing it, nearly obsessively on a loop. The lyrics are in French and 'secret de Polichinelle' is a secret that is known by all but remains hidden. This expression originates from a comedy play in 1903 by the French writer Pierre Wolff.

Triste fête - by Janie

Je l'ai reconnu coupable

Je l'ai vu dans ses yeux

De quoi il était capable

J'ai pas eu besoin d'aveux

Si j'avais su

Si j'avais vu

Ne serait-ce qu'un grain de sable

Si j'avais su

Si j'avais pu lire sur le visage du diable

Que ça faisait des mois, des semaines

Qu'en cachette

Il te faisait une triste fête

On dit que les murs ont des oreilles

Pourquoi n'ont-ils pas entendu

Chacun de tes appels à l'aide

Qui aurait répondu puisque le crime est secret de Polichinelle

Il pourra te faire taire

Je parlerai pour deux

Quels qu'en soient les doutes

Les paroles qu'on enterre

Le prix que ça me coûte

Si j'avais su

Si j'avais vu

Ne serait-ce qu'un grain de sable

Si j'avais su

Si j'avais pu lire sur le visage du diable

On dit que les murs ont des oreilles

Pourquoi n'ont-ils pas entendu

Chacun de tes appels à l'aide

Qui aurait répondu puisque le crime est secret de Polichinelle

Un jour je te promets

Tu aimeras sans mal

Tu feras de tes blessures

Ta plus grande bataille

Et je sais, ô combien

Il te faudra du courage

Mais tu sais, le soleil

Vient juste après l'orage

Dubai, 1985

Chapter Three

The Diagnosis

As described in *Cruelly betrayed*, my mother found herself marrying a man, she never loved. I will never know whether she ever developed feelings for Nicolas. She was let down by her Prince Charming shortly before her dream wedding was meant to take place and suddenly, she was 'rescued' by Nicolas to keep up the good family image. What would people say, after all? Who would want to marry her if the wedding was fully called off? There must have been something wrong with the bride-to-be, right?

As we have seen before, if at the start of a relationship both parties are not on an equal level of emotional, physical, and financial stability, the relationship may be set for disaster. That gap will always cause the more 'stable' party to position him or herself as the 'saviour' and so, despite the emancipation and rebalancing of the 'weaker' party, the 'saviour' will always make the 'weaker' party feel like he or she owes them. If the 'stronger' party is a narcissistic pervert, then there is no chance of the relationship ever becoming healthy. The only way out, is literally out!

My mother had everything to feel fulfilled and yet this life was by far not what she had imagined as a young medical graduate. She had big hopes to travel the world and put her knowledge and skills at the profit of the more vulnerable population in our society. Instead, she felt trapped with a man and six children to take care of. She was a competent doctor and had dreams that reached beyond being a stay-at-home-mother and housewife. Up until then, as far as my memory goes, there was nothing special about my family. My mind as well as the VHS tapes display a normal happy family with both spouses playing their respective roles. My mother was not particularly submissive to her husband despite her being the homemaker and him being the main breadwinner.

Our garden in Remich, in south-eastern Luxembourg, overlooking the river Moselle was idyllic. Up until that point, everything seemed normal, and my childhood was not any more unusual than that of my peers.

The turning point was Mira's birth in 1991. My mother became more and more unhappy with her life, despite seemingly living the dream. She did not recognise herself in the role she was unwillingly meant to play. As the months passed, perhaps accentuated by postpartum depression, she started to question everything, including her accidental marriage to Nicolas. What may have also contributed to her becoming more and more depressed while critically thinking about her life, was her father's unexpected death. It's like him passing gave her the freedom she needed. She had married Nicolas out of desperation, to honour her father's imposed perfect family image. He was very dominant over her. It was a practical deal back then, nothing else. When her father passed away, she suddenly felt a huge sense of relief. She was finally freed from the decade long shackles of pleasing her father and staying married to a man she didn't love.

When Nicolas noticed that his wife was increasingly becoming upset, he evidently became worried. She began rebelling more and more against him and finally asked to get divorced. She mentioned random names of men from her past. Following her father's passing, she finally stood up for herself. She was no longer going to quietly play the role that she had never auditioned for in the first place, only to make her father happy. She was going to do what she felt was the right thing to do for herself and her children. Up until that point, I had never witnessed my father being aggressive towards his wife. Perhaps he was, behind closed doors away from curious children's eyes, I will never know.

When I think back to our time in that white bungalow in Remich, I still have memories of my parents showing affection to one another. My mother was still a mother, a wife, and a 'normal' person. She wore beautiful flowery dresses, put make-up on, displayed pretty jewellery and looked after herself. She had a social life, played with her children in the garden and did not show any 'strange' behaviour. We often had guests at home, and she could have conversations, discuss, debate, and laugh. As a child, I often wished my mother could return to that state. The decades that followed with her being in a chronic semi-dead, sedated state imposed by her husband had fully sucked out the residual life she still had in her. That man should return to prison, only for that. Nicolas is solely responsible for destroying my mother, what a waste of human life.

Nicolas, unable to divert his wife's wish from divorcing him, looked for ways to quieten her. Despite substantial efforts to get her off the idea of breaking up, he did not manage to fully get the upper hand. My mother started writing letters to her deceased father. Nicolas saw that as a 'crazy' action and was starting to question his wife's sanity. Just like the letter I wrote to my deceased mother, a few pages ago, he will be thinking the same about me when he reads this current book. I hope he does. I am just as 'crazy' as my mother. The more he compares me to her, the more satisfaction I get. I am pretty much made up of 100 % maternal DNA.

Nicolas, at his wits' ends, didn't know what to do about the situation, fearing his wife would get through with the divorce. What would the neighbours say? My mother had already sought legal advice and was ready to finally assert herself after playing the 'good girl' all her life, out of fear of disappointing her father. When Nicolas realised that my mother was very serious about splitting up, he asked his family for advice on what to do. On a trip back home to his mother abroad, he got to know, through relatives, that my mother used to have a great aunt called Bethany who was schizophrenic and died in a closed psychiatric facility in Trieste, Italy.

Equipped with this knowledge, upon his return to Luxembourg, Nicolas decided to pack up his whole family in his green Renault break and drive to Trieste. He told his young children, that they were embarking on an adventure. We had no idea what the point of that long trip was, but any trip is exciting for children, especially if sugar-coated as an adventure, so no questions asked. Nicolas was on a quest. He needed some evidence to support what his relatives had insinuated back home. In Italy, we visited numerous institutions, that looked to me like nursing homes, some of them were obviously monasteries.

Without google back then, Nicolas must have had a difficult time locating all the facilities of interest in Trieste. Nicolas wasn't going to give us a briefing on the real purpose of the trip. With his inability to speak Italian and the limited English of the local people, his 'adventure' must have been extra challenging. Finally, after days of searching, he found THE psychiatric hospital, where Bethany was admitted to by her family for the remaining of her life and where she ended up dying at.

Nicolas somehow managed to obtain Bethany's medical records from 1921 stating that she was born in 1873. The Italian typewritten document states that she lacks an objective view on her disease. She seems to have lived in France for a long time and worked as a French teacher in Italy. She has suffered from paranoid delusions over many years. She believes to be the daughter of Napoleon III and Eugenia and develops around this delusion, romantic fantasies, involving royal houses, clericals, freemasons, republicans, Napoleon's cousins, and Orleans enemies. She experiences illogical, maniac and delusional episodes.

Since Bethany was carrying the same surname as my mother, Nicolas could then easily retrieve these archives. Back in Luxembourg, he did not hesitate to pay a visit to a psychiatrist. I have no idea, how much of this was strategic and ill-intentioned and how much was genuine care for his wife. With tangible evidence at hand, he supported his suspicions of hereditary schizophrenia to convince the psychiatrist to prescribe the first ever anti-psychotics, that my mother ended up remaining on until her death. Most likely, she was not even present at that consultation. Since Nicolas was a pharmacist himself, he had a broad knowledge of the medications available and could therefore throw in jargon, here and there, in the conversation to boost his credibility in the eyes of the healthcare professionals.

I honestly don't know how Nicolas managed to get these first pills into my mother. In the early days, she was not given the thigh injections. I can only assume that he hid the pills into her drink or food. Since he used to do that later on and even instruct his children to hide the drugs in our mother's tea or food, I can only imagine that he wouldn't have hesitated for a single second.

As the months passed, my mother became more and more 'rebellious' against her husband who was not agreeing to go through with the divorce she desperately wanted. What would his family say, after all? A good Christian couple does not divorce, ever. Nicolas was very careful to portray the 'perfect family', regardless of the price to pay. Someone would always have to pay; in this case it was definitely my mother. Returning from school one day, our father asked us to pack our clothes as we were about to embark on a new adventure. When we asked where our mother was, he told us that she took the plane to spend some time abroad. I didn't understand where she went and why she left us.

All I remember is that the three eldest children were driven to Paris, while the three youngest children, baby included, were taken elsewhere. Andreas, Denise, and I lived with Nicolas' sister Sally on the outskirts of Paris. That family was extremely Catholic, and four out of five children ended up becoming devoted priests, nuns and monks. We suddenly found ourselves away from our parents and three younger siblings, not understanding what we were doing in a foreign country, radically taken out of school. With the months passing and no solution to my mother's 'problem' in sight, Sally started looking for a primary school for us. We could not speak any French and we were indoctrinated in this extremist family, never to return to Luxembourg again. I had no idea what the relatives were doing to my mother abroad and what the future held.

I just remember absolutely hating being in that family. Living in a small apartment, Sally found herself looking after eight children, three of them, not 'Catholic' enough and so, she and her husband put in an extra effort to convert these three unwanted children. My uncle was very violent, and he would whip us all with his belt, whether the children were his or not. We once received a good whipping because we dared to go out on the balcony on New Year's Eve to watch the fireworks. That was not Christian enough. What would Jesus say if he saw us standing there all excited about the coloured sparks?

I have no idea how long we spent with that crazy family in Paris, but it was way too long for my taste. Children don't have a concept of time, thankfully. One day, out of nowhere, Nicolas came to rescue us. Naively, we thought we would be going back to Remich. We had missed many months of school. Instead, Nicolas took us to our mother abroad and I had no idea how she had spent the past months and whether harm had been done to her. She seemed as unhappy and unfazed as I had seen her last before being separated from her. Perhaps the medication was starting to 'work' and she was well on her way to becoming the vegetable that her husband intended.

Many months later, we found ourselves back in Luxembourg, but had to change schools without any explanations. I was too young to understand what these adults were up to. All I know, is that wherever Nicolas went, we had to follow. Children are always the victims of their parents' actions. Trying his best to keep my mother away from the divorce idea, Nicolas started to look for new ways to sedate his wife on a regular basis. She had to keep quiet and not be an interference. That inconvenience needed to be kept under control. It was now 1992, one year following Mira's birth and Nicolas had fully convinced several psychiatrists based on Bethany's records and my mother's 'crazy' letters that she was schizophrenic as there was 'proof' of a family history of the disease. 1992 is also the year that Nicolas, out of the blue, one night came into my bed and molested me.

What came first? The chicken or the egg? Did my mother become sick because she saw that Nicolas had been hurting her daughter or did Nicolas know that she knew and therefore, started admitting her to the psychiatric hospital? Did he admit her and suddenly find an opportunity to sexually abuse me? I honestly have no idea but all I know is that my mother was not sick, merely depressed, just like any human being would have been in her situation, stuck with that man. Many questions will forever remain a mystery.

Once sick, always sick. After the issue of the first prescription of anti-psychotics, it was an easy game for Nicolas to have repeat prescriptions without the need for justification or even the presence of my mother at the consultation. He was pulling the strings from then on. He could hold the exclusive control over another human being. For a narcissistic pervert, this is the ultimate satisfaction. He could do whatever he wanted with his wife and his children. He could move the pawns however he wanted.

He could legally drug his wife, facilitated by the psychiatrists, who had no idea who they were dealing with. A narcissistic pervert is hard to spot. Nicolas was the charismatic caring husband and father of six adorable children. Who would ever suspect that his intentions were nothing but love-filled? Meanwhile, he was molesting his eldest daughter and with absolute freedom, realised how easy it was to get away with his crimes. Everyone saw, nobody hindered him.

Evidently, my mother was not going to let him have the upper hand over her. She had finally seen his true face and what he was capable of and so, despite being drugged, she could still gather some energy to drive Nicolas utterly mad. She became an interference on purpose. Was she pretending to be sick to keep him away from me? I'd love to believe so. Since I am convinced that she was not sick at all, my theory goes in the direction of trying to protect me with the little energy she had left while being under the influence. The dose and potency of which, only increased over the years as she always needed stronger medication to achieve the desired silencing effect.

Documented in the medical archives, I can chronologically follow my mother's hell. She was first admitted in 1992 by police force. This event was very spectacular, especially for us children to watch from afar. We could not fully comprehend what was going on and what exactly our mother's 'crime' was for the police to turn up. Our father was adamant that this was necessary and so, we believed him and conformed. He explained to us from then on, that our mother was not like other mothers. He said that she was 'sick' and that she needed to be taken care of at the hospital as she was not complying with the prescribed medication at home.

He said that he was now both mother and father. He would be taking care of us and slowly made us feel that he was sacrificing everything he had for our good despite our mother being ill. We should no longer believe anything our mother says as she's 'crazy' and therefore she must take these pills that she refuses. When the patriarchy says so, then there was no discussing, right?

Before every ambulance pick-up, he would make sure his children knew THE exact reason for her to be taken away. It's like he was brainwashing us so that we repeat the script when the psychiatrist asks us at the hospital. He needed to make sure that his game was spotless.

Over the years, my mother has been admitted to the psychiatric hospital numerous times, each time initiated by her husband. The first hospitalisation occurred following a violent interaction. She says that her husband hits her regularly. He denies it and says his wife is crazy and visits a nursing home, convinced she has seen her mother. This was one year after she was first prescribed powerful medication for a disease she never suffered from. Did these drugs possibly alter her perceptions? Did she play along and pretend to be 'crazy'? She tells the nurse that in her past life, she was deeply in love with a man, that she still feels exists in her heart and mind. She also says that she used to work as a doctor in Dubai and could often heal her patients without the use of medicine.

Her husband specifies that she's been prescribed antipsychotics abroad. The nurse notes that my mother was so tired after this conversation that she just fell into her bed. A few days following her admission, my mother was behaving very calmly and was still hoping that someone would come and pick her up from the hospital. She is, however, told that her husband thinks it would be best for everyone if she remains in the psychiatry and that he shouldn't visit too often. The documents often state the symptomatology of the disease based on my father's accounts rather than the observations from the medical staff. Of course, his accounts never omit to mention the hereditary schizophrenia.

According to him, my mother showed impulsive behaviour, refused to take the prescribed antipsychotics, and put herself and others in danger with her provocative attitude. She laughs too much and was very agitated. Her thoughts were confusing. She was focusing on a lover from her past with hallucinations as reported by her husband. She is also convinced to have healing power. The patient does not understand that she is sick and therefore is classified as being non-compliant when it comes to taking her medication, aimed at bringing her back to reality. The discharge letter states that the husband has not come to visit at all during his wife's hospitalisation and that she only received visits from her mother and brother. My mother has repeatedly insisted to be released prematurely and since there was no further reason to keep her locked up, she was allowed to leave the hospital against her husband's refusal.

Sometimes, Nicolas would tell us that we were going on a family trip. My mother would be very excited and get it in the car. Unbeknownst to her, Nicolas had prepared a suitcase with her belongings and the 'day trip' was him driving her to the psychiatric hospital for another long stay, without her consent; fooling her like you wouldn't even dare tricking a child. In his eyes, she was his possession and had been all along. He has never considered her as a fellow human being.

Another day, another admission letter states that my mother has destroyed furniture and tried to kill her husband with a knife and therefore needs to be forcibly hospitalised. She is said to be delirious and that she doesn't understand that she is sick. It is said that her psychotic condition is deteriorating despite the medication given. She is described as aggressive, supposedly threatens her husband and therefore is a danger to others.

The medical folder is filled with police letters requesting the hospitalisation against my mother's will, even requiring the mayor's approval before each admission. With thirty years of admissions, one can imagine the thickness of this folder. It looks more like a criminal record than a horror story of my lovely mother, who had been suffering in silence for all these years. She had no voice left. All the reports mention her husband. He is omnipresent. He says that she does not want to voluntarily be admitted to the psychiatric hospital and always runs away whenever he tells her that they will be driving there.

On admission, my mother is said to not resist, she is generally happy and always smiling. She tells the nurse that there is a big difference between her and her husband. She says that she does not understand why her husband gets her admitted after she cooked a meal, only because she mixed different ingredients like bell peppers and tomatoes. She says her husband is very nervous and that he always buys the cheapest food. She speaks about the Holy Spirit. She says she wants to send it to someone to protect her from evil. She refuses to take her medication. She then mentions her husband and says *there is a story about him I need to tell you.* The nurse writes that when she returned to listen to the story, the patient had already fallen asleep. As a diagnosis, the nurse writes *deteriorating chronic paranoid psychosis,* adding *permanent familial conflict* underneath it.

In another document, it is said that Nicolas has asked for financial support to hire a cleaning lady to help him with his six children while his wife is hospitalised. With regards to this request, the author writes that her colleague has told her not to send an assistant there, as the familial situation is complicated and that she doesn't trust the patient's husband because he often shows very bizarre reactions.

Another day, another admission letter states that my mother was brought in by police force, yet again. She had been hiding in a garden shed in the neighbouring town since the night before and she was escorted to the hospital by policemen who kept her tightly fastened in an ambulance stretcher so that she could not move.

The following morning, she was calm and did not resist, she was kind and smiley. Her husband and children came to visit her. Two weeks later, she doesn't speak anymore, helps with the chores and is very cooperative. She has low expectations and is happy with the minimum. Two weeks have passed again, and she planned on going to the swimming pool with her husband and children. Her husband, however, has brought her back early to the hospital. He said that she became aggressive with him in the car and wanted to flee. He said that she thought that he was bringing her to the airport like last time to get rid of her. My sweet mother was already suffering from PTSD by then and lived in constant fear because of one man's barbaric actions.

Another day, another admission letter states that my mother has arrived at the hospital in company of the police. She had another violent argument with her husband, who says that she has threatened him. The husband declares that she doesn't look after their common children and neglects the household. She refuses to be injected with the antipsychotic and tells the nurse that she wants to stay at the hospital for a few days as she can't tolerate being around her husband anymore. She needs to rest as he's making her life very difficult. The patient is behaving very quietly and shows no distinct symptoms.

Two weeks later, the husband visits with their children and asks the doctors to make sure that his wife must get her 'every right to decide' revoked. He says she urgently needs to be put under his guardianship, as she insists on getting a divorce from him. He says that he needs to keep this marriage intact against his wife's wish, for the sake of their children. A few days after that visit, my mother tells the nurse that she wants to emigrate to Canada, where her mother lives and doesn't want to stay in Luxembourg with her husband and children. Another month passes and her husband picks her up.

A radiology report shows that my mother has broken ribs, probably from a past fracture. With the clear evidence of physical violence from her husband, why would this report remain without further action against her husband? I am really trying to understand this.

Another day, another admission letter states that this time, my mother has behaved inadequately at home. She has bought too many groceries, did not do her household chores, sent all her money to her brother, neglected her children, and MASSIVELY threatened her husband and off she goes for another long stay amongst patients, who are there for the right reasons. Perhaps, many of them have been dubbed 'crazy' by a relative because they were an inconvenience? Who knows how many of these patients are really belonging there?

The letter says that my mother was very stressed at admission and the team could not communicate with her. The patient did not understand that she was sick and refused any further examination and medication. Over the next days and weeks, my mother was calm and did not seek contact with her fellow patients. She was passive and did not take part in the group activities. Instead, she spent her days, sitting in an armchair, staring into the emptiness through the window. She was still non-compliant and therefore she was forcibly given the injection against her will, with her four limbs tightly fastened.

Over the next days, her state improved. Side note, what exactly was her state before if the document mentions that she is calm and quiet and her only 'sign' of disease was for her to be sadly staring through the window. My God, what was she supposed to do instead? Be grateful to be locked up only based on lies perpetrated by her devil husband? Was she supposed to jump up in joy and interact with her fellow patients? Was she expected to participate in the group activities despite her being totally sane and feeling the injustice in her deepest core? Who would be 'happy' being in her situation? If you ask me, being upset, passive, lethargic and depressed while staring through a window would be exactly what I would have most likely done too, had I been stuck in this place.

The report concludes that following further improvement of my mother's state and after discussion with her husband, the procedure of guardianship has been started. It also says that she finally 'understands' that she is sick and was therefore released from hospital again. Of course, being in her situation, at some point, I would also have just complied and pretended to really be sick to shut everyone up. I would most likely have played that game too if every opposition from my side was in vain and I understood that this was my only chance of getting out of this prison to return to live with my children. I would have agreed to everything in the end as showing resistance would have kept me locked up for longer.

We are now at the seventh admission within a few years and the police letter states that my mother has destroyed furniture and tried to kill my father using a hammer this time. Who knows, perhaps she was protecting me after seeing him abuse me; I really don't know, but I can't describe the joy and satisfaction I feel reading about these murder attempts! Seemingly, Nicolas also told the police that my mother tried to blow up the house by fiddling with the gas appliance. The last sentence states that her six children live in that house after all, that she is a danger to herself and her surrounding after threatening her husband.

My mother is then transported to the hospital by the local police and when asked, she answers that her husband was violent with her. She is described as calm, collaborating and her conversation very structured. She tells the nurse that her husband has been very violent for six years and that he tried to poison her with drugs. She says that he regularly puts drugs in her food, thinking she doesn't notice. The nurse writes that the couple is currently divorcing.

My mother has often left the hospital by signing a waiver, that she is responsible for herself, and the hospital can't bear responsibility for any consequences arising from this discharge. One day, after signing such a waiver, Nicolas made sure to admit her the next day, as she surprisingly turned up at home without his permission. To justify his wish with arguments as this time my mother didn't even get the chance to do 'wrong' at home, he wrote a letter to her doctor which reads:

I am Nicolas. I request the neuropsychiatric hospital to keep and retain my wife Nelly for a minimum period of 3 months, because:

- *She is hereditarily sick (schizophrenia)*

- *She always refuses to take treatment at home*

- *Her behaviour is just too happy and euphoric, never serious.*

Please put in consideration:

a) I have six children and it is too difficult for me to control them if their mother is at home

b) When she is at the hospital, my children are very well behaved and obey all my orders, so that I can construct their personalities

c) My wife is just a careless mother, which can be risky for the whole family. For example, she put water in the gas appliance, which could have caused a house fire. Also, many many other actions, but too difficult for me to say.

Signed Nicolas

...and my mother was readmitted to the hospital one day after signing her waiver and solely based on her husband's request.

In the same year, a few months later, there was another police admission letter. This time, my mother's 'crime' was described as follows: *The woman is aggressive. Her husband showed us the kitchen, where the woman mixed an excessive amount of ingredients in the mixer.*

Nine years on and way too many hospital admissions later, Nicolas writes a four-page letter to the psychiatrist, in the hope of making the hospital keep his wife for as long as possible. If he could, he would have signed an admission request for life for my mother, not thinking twice about it.

Dear Dr. K,

I have received a telephone call from a doctor at your clinic, who said I should take my wife back home as per your orders. Please Dr. K., at the moment, truly, I am very stressed, I cannot tolerate the situation anymore.

For the following reasons:

1. *On the 30th May, in the morning, my wife got up at 3am and switched the TV on. At 7:30, my son Leonard asked his mother for his gym bag. She was just laughing; he became angry and shouted at her. I promised him to look for it and to bring it to school. I looked for it and gave it to him (my wife had displaced it on the top of a cupboard). I called Dr. M. to come home and give my wife the injection. Nelly heard me speaking to Dr. M. and took the phone off me, threw it away and started*

hitting me. She tried to break my glasses, violently ripped my clothes despite me doing my best to control her. I phoned Dr. M. again, for him to come as soon as possible to give her the injection, but he said 'No'. He said she should go to the hospital straight away and this is what happened.

2. My children are currently preparing for their final exams of the year.

3. I chose to work from home to give my wife and children more time with me.

4. My children and I are truly very sad about having my wife at your clinic and we discuss the situation together daily to try to find a solution. Every time, my wife is hospitalised for a few weeks at your clinic, she becomes perfect and always promises to continue taking the medicine, but she never fulfils her promise. She only takes the tranquiliser and the sleeping pill and blood pressure medicine. Therefore, one month after she comes back home, she's back again to her disease which shows the following character:

- She damages furniture

- She tries to repair or invent an electrical appliance and puts herself at risk of an electric shock as her ideas are illogical.

- She cleans the kitchen appliances with water.

- I pay around 10,000 Luxembourgish francs for gas every month, while not getting use from the heating because my wife:

- Opens all the windows at home, in the summer or winter, she doesn't like the hot climate but my children like it, especially in the winter
- She always turns down the heating in the house
- She changes the settings of the heating system in the basement

- She does not recycle correctly
- She flooded my shower
- She cleans the wooden floor with the wrong cleaning product
- She cleans the sink with the wrong product

5. Washing clothes

   a. She uses the wrong laundry product

   b. She never checks the pockets before washing clothes. She washed my important papers, coins, or paper tissues. She once washed 60,000 Luxembourgish francs. Another time, she washed my check book. I discovered that at midnight, on my way to Monaco by car to buy stamps.

   c. She often washes all the clothes at the wrong temperature and mixes all the colours, often *the clothes become shorter in size.*

6. *If she's allowed to cook, she doesn't cook properly:*

    a. *She doesn't defrost the frozen food correctly*

    b. *She uses too many spices or salt when she cooks*

    c. *She prepares too much food, which then needs to be frozen.*

7. *My wife never wants to have an animal at home.*

Dear Dr. K.,

Because of all of that, I have no alternative than to:

- *Close the windows with wires*

- *Lock the kitchen (with key and digital pin code)*

- *Block the heating with a special key*

- *Lock all the doors of the house when she is alone at home.*

- *The keys of the kitchen and the other rooms are always kept with one of my children, but the problem is that my wife becomes aggressive and asks my children to give her the key to the kitchen. Then they are afraid and give it to her. Then, she does whatever she wants in the kitchen, including cooking.*

- *Control my wife when she drinks coffee*

- *Wash and iron clothes myself when I have time.*

- *Every child locks his or her bedroom, so their mother can't touch anything.*

Therefore, I request your kindness to take care of my wife until the summer. After that, no problem, she can return home under one condition: very strong system to take her prescribed medicine regularly, otherwise we will go back to the starting point.

Nicolas made Andreas and me sign the above letter against our mother. Both of us were still teenagers at that point.

A document that keeps showing its face in the heavy medical folder, is the medical report from my mother's great-aunt, stating that she was schizophrenic and died in a psychiatric hospital in Italy. Year after year, like a game of Broken Telephone, the false information has travelled across my mother's medical history. On Bethany's report, we falsely read in handwritten capital letters 'Patient's grand-mother'. This infamous Italian report will forever be known as the basis, on which a wrong diagnosis of schizophrenia was given to my mother. This medical report will forever be known for the beginning of the unimaginable hell that my mother had to go through.... all alone.

Another document strikes me with her handwriting, signed with Dr. N.S. She is essentially begging the psychiatrist to give her sleeping pills as she is suffering from chronic insomnia. I can physically feel her pain. Both our extreme insomnia was perpetrated by the same sadist, while he sleeps peacefully night after night. How unfair that both of us fell victim to this perverted man at the same time, with the same consequences on our health. Currently, going through another PTSD-induced phase of incurable insomnia, I am reminded of the injustice. I am paying my whole life for the actions of a pervert thirty years prior. The suffering does not end when the abuse stops. It's an internal dormant slow brewing distress, that shows its ugly face decades after the actual crime has ended.

The anxiety has become a part of me and it's a constant battle to try to keep the upper hand day in and day out. I refuse to let the sick actions of this monster define the rest of my life and rob me of my happiness. Sometimes I manage, other days, it's hard to win this mental and physical battle of PTSD.

Okay, let me recapitulate, you know, just to understand. My mother is admitted to a psychiatric hospital using police force and an ambulance after her husband tells the police that she has tried to hurt him and their children. Of course, first she is put down with a potent depressant injection in her thigh, like an unruly animal, when she tries to show resistance. Then, Nicolas tells the medical team a long story about how my mother's aunt was ALSO schizophrenic and that my mother inherited that from her. Credible enough for the medical team to repeat that story in each report. My mother then finds herself imprisoned with real psychiatric patients and is expected to just sit still and pretend that this is totally fine.

Not being able to defend herself against her husband's convincing charismatic charade, she has absolutely no chance. With each admission, with each prescription, the schizophrenia label on her forehead gets stickier while the image of the caring, sweet husband and father gets reinforced. I mean, how would I feel and behave, had someone done the same with me? I would most likely also show defiance if I was repeatedly injected with strong drugs to keep me quiet. Let's not forget that my only 'crime' would be cooking the wrong dish or moving furniture. I would also defend myself if policemen treated me this aggressively. I would also have run away if they had tried to catch me to get me locked up in a hospital filled with actual delusional patients. The powers were so unequal. Then, imagine being told by the medical team that I don't understand that I am 'sick' and therefore labelled as uncooperative.

My God, imagine being in that horror movie. Imagine being totally sane and stuck in this place with professionals treating you as if you were insane, only based on the convincing account of a relative. I can only assume that with each year that passes in this state, I would genuinely become mad as I would either give up trying to convince people that I am not crazy or perhaps the potent drugs would really alter my perceptions, to the point of being detached from the person I was before this hell started. I can't imagine my words not bearing any credibility while the person at the source of my trials and tribulations, is being believed at face value.

My poor mother. How awful it must have been for her, to be on her own in her agony. I doubt an invented horror movie could be this intense. A scriptwriter would never be able to invent such a perverted story. This current book will be turned into a movie one day. It's authentic and thrilling, because it concerns real people and not fictional characters.

How unfair and cruel this situation was. How vile can a man be to destroy a beautiful soul like this and still get away with it? An analogy comes to mind. It's like having surgery, open heart, if you will and you're being operated on. You can feel and hear everything, every cut and every twist. You can't talk or voice your pain. The surgical team continues to operate, talking about you and think the anaesthesia is fully working, but it isn't at all. Let that sink in, for a minute. This happened to me during my first c-section. I, however, was still able to scream out of pain and let the surgeons know that I could feel everything and that neither the epidural nor the spinal block had worked on me.

The reports repeatedly mention that my mother is 'dangerous'. This is the total opposite image of how I have perceived her all my life. The only person who thought she was dangerous was Nicolas, as she was dangerous in the sense that she could reveal how he had been sexually abusing his daughter over the years. She could have been the one to send him to prison for life, so it was best to keep her as passive and totally dead on the inside as possible. I have never felt that she could have hurt me or any of my siblings, therefore these reports are even more astonishing as I have never associated the word 'danger' with my mother. She was the impersonation of kindness and gentleness, therefore also the perfect prey for her narcissistic pervert of a husband.

She had absolutely no chance to get out of this vicious cycle as the system was being fooled by this manipulator repeatedly, smooth strategy. Improvised? Opportunistic? Planned? I have no idea, but it obviously worked brilliantly for him to get conveniently and regularly rid of my mother.

One of the most unbelievable discoveries in this folder is the fact that following a psychiatric expertise, the court had ordered a social enquiry into my family, because of indications of violence and abuse. Over 5 years, there were ELEVEN reminders sent from the judge to the responsible service. Not one person has bothered checking what was going on in our house despite obvious suspicions about Nicolas.

I need an apology from the state, I need recognition that someone somewhere massively messed up by his or her incompetence with unbearable consequences for both my mother and me. I need to be heard and my pain acknowledged. How many victims have been in the same position? How do I know this gross negligence is not causing victims today to remain in the hands of their criminal? This can't be, especially that in my case, there were mentions of sexual abuse of minors in the documents, I mean how much more explicit does one need to be? My case was an easy one as it went on over years and there were so many blatant signs and yet, the enablers allowed my abuser to continue unhindered.

Sutton, UK, 1986

Chapter Four

The Hospital Ward

From the endless handwritten diaries from the medical staff, I have been able to extract many heart-breaking accounts but also plenty of soothing ones.

...sitting in her room, she is staring into the emptiness through the window.

...she looks sad and doesn't take part in the group activities.

...she is not expressing any delirious or bizarre statements.

...she spent the whole day in her room.

...she has been behaving calmly so far. She just wants to be discharged as soon as possible.

...she can't sleep without medication; this has been her only request during her stay.

...she spoke to her children on the phone today.

...she wants to spend the weekend at home with her children but did not get permission from her doctor...

...she participated in the workshop today; she was

making a necklace but stopped after 15 minutes because her son came.

...she speaks quietly, she hasn't looked through the window today.

...she prays a lot, talks about her family situation, she says her husband makes her furious and then gets her admitted to the psychiatric hospital. After a while, she returns home and everything is fine, she says she forgives him for treating her this way.

...today she comes accompanied by her son; again, following a violent interaction with her husband. She is known to the hospital as a chronic patient with deteriorating schizophrenic psychosis.

...her husband has had enough...

...her husband called. He informed us that his wife had not taken any medication when she was at home and that we should particularly keep an eye on her.

...the patient is angry because she is refused to go outside alone for a walk. She says that her husband is dead to her; she never wants to see him again.

...she stopped talking, except with the 'elderly ladies' on the floor. She likes to have a walk with them in silence. She doesn't want contact with the medical team.

...she has permission to go outside on her own. She was seen packing her suitcase; informs us that she will not be coming back as she needs to go home to her children. Her husband is supposedly going to travel, and she *doesn't want the nanny to be alone with her children.*

...she shows me flight tickets for herself; showing that she will be going to Spain on her own in two weeks. She signed a waiver and went home on her own responsibility.

...the patient came again by ambulance to the hospital after returning home only yesterday.

...her husband called and was furious because we let her go by signing a waiver. He said she will be readmitted today, which then happened.

...she said that she was cleaning at home and suddenly the ambulance came to take her. She went with them without resistance as she sees her stay at the hospital as a holiday, but her only worry is who is going to look after her children as her husband is travelling soon.

...Dr K. came today shortly but didn't prescribe any medication and did not understand why she was back at the hospital without her doing anything wrong at home.

...the patient says not to cash in the check that she has left with us.

...the husband came and signed the admission request

...the patient does not want any antipsychotic medication. She has now been informed that she is back for another admission, and she says that's ok for her but hopes she can return home to look after her children.

...despite her relaxed attitude, she started tearing up when she talked about her children...

...she now agrees to be injected with the antipsychotic drug...

...today she received a visit and refuses any further medicine. She asks why she is being prescribed tranquilisers as she has always been a calm person. She is indeed calm and quiet.

...she is kind and relaxed, but feels uneasy because she misses her children...

...she has helped in the workshop, has painted, and done crafts; she seemingly had fun.

...a visit from Dr. K, who says that if her husband comes, she can have a walk with him.

...she took part in the baking activity; she appeared to have loved it. She asked the staff when she didn't know what to do next in the recipe and was visibly happy about her results.

...she is frightened because she must sleep on her own...

...she is also afraid of Mrs S. as she slapped her the other day.

...she needs a medical certificate because she has a holiday booked in a week's time.

...today she did a sewing activity; she's feeling fine.

...the patient is readmitted. According to her husband,

she mixed food worth 12,000 Luxembourgish Francs.

...constant disobedience towards her husband. She has been mixing food for weeks - sugar, vegetables, spices. Her husband says she only laughs. He says she gets more and more bizarre, aggressive and does not take her neuroleptics.

...transport by ambulance and police to the hospital. She was nervous and still doesn't accept that she is sick, but she is cooperative.

...she is calm and compliant. She shows no strange behaviour, she looks pensively through the window. She wants to go home as soon as possible.

...she hasn't really socialised with her fellow patients. She sits in her room or by the window. She shows no symptom whatsoever and has visibly adapted to the situation.

...she seems very meditative...

...she helped in the kitchen this evening. When she needs something, she asks, but otherwise doesn't seek social contact.

...her husband and four out of six children visited today. She has tried to convince her husband to go back home with them, but her husband explained to us in detail how she causes total chaos at home.

...that she wakes the children up early at 5 am to revise before school, then she makes breakfast but mixes everything wrongly together; he says she does not obey.

...she cleaned the wooden floor with the wrong product. She turns the heating on and opens the windows. She cleans the pavement in the winter, which then gets icy.

..she gives her children's toys and clothes to other relatives as a gift without asking. She paints the wall and doesn't finish the job.

...the husband hired a nanny, but when he came home from work, his wife had been drinking tea with her instead of doing what she was hired for. He says there are too many things so it is impossible for him to list everything.

...he says that he might as well get divorced, look for a new wife and live a quiet life with his children and his new wife without the disturbance of his current wife.

...he says once he is married again, Nelly could just come to visit his new family sometimes and work as a doctor again...the patients loved her.

...her husband states that he is currently putting his house in order. He and the six children were apparently locking themselves up when the mother was home.

...for the sake of the children, he says he needs to keep the mother at a distance. He is scared that they get impacted by the situation.

...he adds that his wife's behaviour causes him to regularly call the police to take her away, in front of the neighbours.

...he says that the neighbours and the children see their

mother as crazy and don't want anything to do with her anymore...

...he has had enough of his wife terrorising everyone and destroying the house...especially because she refuses medication.

...she is waiting for her husband to pick her up, but the nurses can't reach him by phone.

...she wants to be kept busy, today she washed the dishes in the kitchen...

...today, she went to the post office accompanied by staff, to cash in a cheque.

...her husband has agreed to discharge her, under one condition, that she receives her injection...

...a readmission, the patient has been very aggressive towards her husband. When he called the doctor to come home to give her the injection, she refused any medication.

...according to her husband, she doesn't manage the household chores. He has to cook, clean and iron for his children

...the children are <u>very scared</u>

...she received a visit from her husband and children today...the husband says he doesn't want her to come back home.

...she went for a walk with the group. She is happy to

be in the fresh air; she does not socialise within the group...

...she needs to be convinced to take part in the group activities, tends to choose group activities that take place outdoors.

...she has become very reserved, has no contact with other patients...

...today, she received a phone call from her daughter, she was visibly very nervous during the whole conversation...

...despite the staff calling her husband several times, he was unreachable and there was no contact at all from his side. The patient advises to call the local police to check on her children, to make sure everything is fine.

...the husband finally called and refuses to take his wife back home. He will talk to Dr. K. on Monday, in order to prolong her stay.

...she is convinced her husband will pick her up today.

...the husband came in the afternoon with a daughter, who was going on holiday, and she wanted to say goodbye to her mother. The husband has left a four-page letter for Dr. K, to justify why his wife better stay in the hospital for longer and not return home.

...she helped with the meal preparation; she did not ask for help...

...she feels very upset, feels rejected by her husband...

...she complained about Mr. M's behaviour during the night. He entered her room many times when she was asleep. She wants to lock the door from the inside. I told her it is dangerous.

...she complains about Mr. M's nightly visits and fears his threats...

...she is angry that Dr. K listens more to her husband than to her.

...sometimes, she becomes assertive with her statements...

...she tried contacting her brother, for him to pick her up...

...she is very quiet and reserved...

...she asked a nurse to stay with her tonight, as she is scared that Mr. M will come into her room at night. I told her this is not possible, but she should alert the staff immediately if he comes.

...9pm: phone call from her husband...he is very irritated and angry because his wife has told him about Mr. M's behaviour from the previous nights. He wanted to speak to Mr. M himself, but I refused...

...I informed her husband that we will be doing our best to keep Mr. M out of his wife's room tonight...

...the patient is very worried, because her room neighbour is away for the weekend, and she fears sleeping alone...

...11pm: phone call from her husband...he is very worried about his wife; he asks us to look after her and to make sure she is safe...

...we reassure him that she can always come to us if she gets disturbed by Mr. M during the night...

...the patient received her injection on the 6th floor and was taken by force to the lower floor because there was no way we could keep her in isolation and tightened without her consent.

...came out of isolation, had dinner and a shower...

...she tells Dr. K. that her husband hits her regularly. She is calm and behaves adaptively.

...she had a long interview with the nurse. She does not understand that she is sick. She is very affective and emotional. She thinks she is here at the hospital to be physically examined.

...she says that since her father died ten years ago, her husband has abused her. He is very aggressive and hits her. She also mentions that she hits him back. She really wants to return home.

...she asks me to call her husband because he doesn't listen to her. She says that he treats her like a child and asked if we could tell him to bring her clothes.

...she spends most days in bed. She is upset because she can't go home but we explained why this was not possible...

...she is reserved and only talks to her room neighbour

...she says she wanted to get divorced and had already been to the lawyer, but her husband refused and keeps hitting her. She says that they are not a couple but live together like brother and sister

...she can't imagine going to a women's shelter on her own...

...during meals, she does not talk to her fellow patients, has very good table manners...she always eats quickly and goes back to her room and stays in bed under her blanket...

...difficult patient, makes life difficult for her husband and children...

...she is discrete, anxious, polite and isolates herself from the group. She spends her days in bed... the priority now is to motivate and stimulate her to participate in the daily activities

...she wants to return home, she does not understand why she is being kept in a psychiatric hospital...

...the patient has asked to take part in the group activities. She decided to do the Mandala. She needed help with the first steps but could do it by herself afterwards.

...the patient did not find the right location of the material when it was time to end the activity.

...the patient took part in the pantomime activity;

she recognised the different characteristics and could represent them correctly. She said the activity was easy, however, she wrongly believed that her pantomime was always understood by the other patients

...she played a game called 'City-Country-River'. She needed a lot of help and was still unsure; her general knowledge was compromised.

...the patient did not manage to perform simple calculations in her head, she needed to write them all down to be able to get the correct answer.

...she had a great deal of fun playing Skittles, was very enthusiastic and kept asking about her score. She did not, however, seek social contact with the other patients...

...she was eager to achieve a good score, she was very focused.

...the patient is very concerned that she is not being given a sleeping aid, she is suffering from chronic insomnia.

...she seems sad despite being told that she will be returning home for the weekend.

...she needed to be woken up by force...

...she often deforms reality; she says that her husband is responsible for her situation...she does not want to take responsibility for herself and finally accept that she is sick...

...she is still against her husband, feels angry with him for locking her up for no reason...she plays the victim and isolates herself...

...she takes part in a projection of photos from Mauritania and is very fascinated. She asks many questions.

...today, the patient has taken initiative and put make-up on one of her fellow patients. They both enjoyed it. This activity did not last long before the patient returned to her chair to sit there passively...

...the patient is suffering more and more from her chronic insomnia.

...the patient received her injection; she did not show resistance.

...Dr. K. informs the patient that she will now be allowed to go home but only as a test phase to see whether she will behave at home with her husband and children. Otherwise, she will need to be readmitted....

...patient excessively watches TV and feels very exhausted

...the husband brings the patient back after the weekend home. He says it went well.

...patient informs that she is happy because the weekend at home went well. She is looking forward to the next time she is allowed to return home for the weekend, and even more to be allowed to return home for good.

109

...the patient is smiley, friendly, confident and calm.

...the cause of her insomnia will now be investigated.

.... the patient is in a good mood, she participated in the basketball game. Joe said that she is a good player.

...she plays cards in the evening...

...the patient can't wait for her husband to arrive and to take her home for the weekend.

...the husband was supposed to pick her up at 14h but did not turn up. He is apparently abroad.

...the patient begs to return home on Sunday then, only for one day.

...the patient becomes very impatient, because the husband has not picked her up yet...

...after several discussions, the husband finally came and the patient was very happy to go home for a day.

...she is upset to be returning to the hospital. She says she needs to be close to her children and that they need her.

...the patient is sad that her children can't visit her this week because they have exams.

...the husband refuses to let his wife return home but agrees to have a test phase. He tells us that he will be calling the police again if she does not comply and takes her medication.

...she speaks about her traumas; especially the regular violence from her husband, she says that this is the sole source of her chronic insomnia.

...she informs me about the extreme violence of her husband towards her and that it has horrible consequences on her health.

...she seems relieved to have talked about her painful experiences. She is smiley and relaxed, however, stays away from the other patients.

...she spent her day looking out the window, with no contact to the staff or patients.

...she enjoyed the swimming activity...she did not have adequate clothing on her...

...the patient is lying in bed most of the time, under the blanket... she needs to be motivated to participate in the group activities; politely respects the instructions.

...visit from her husband and son. The patient overheard that the husband wants to keep her at the hospital; was upset and went back to her room. The visit lasted only 20 minutes...

...the husband informs us that his wife never loved him, that she got married to him by accident, that she never wanted children, that she always kept him at a distance...

...he says that she wanted to have an abortion during each pregnancy...the daughter remains emotionless during this conversation...apparently, the patient *didn't feel any motherly affection for her children and did not care about them...*

...Dr. M tries to make the patient understand that she is suffering from a psychiatric disease, that makes her relationship with her family difficult, but the patient refuses to believe her...

...she is upset because her husband makes all the decisions on her behalf...

...she is aggressive and seems detached from her issues... blames her husband for everything...a real dialogue of the deaf...

...the patient says we must not believe everything that her husband tells us. She says that he lies and completely discredits her.

...she talks about the difficulties she has with her husband...

...received visit from her brother and his wife. They both tell me that her husband is fully to blame for the patient's deteriorating health...

...they say that the husband often changes the electronic code of the different doors in the house, so that the patient can't even access the kitchen to cook...

...the patient wants to return home as soon as possible, despite her husband being violent to her...she says she can't live without him...

...today, the patient says that she definitely wants to get a divorce...

...she received a visit from a woman, who the patient describes as her husband's lover...

...the patient is sitting in the ping-pong room on a bike, crying...when I asked her why she was upset, she said that everyone here as well as her own family is against her...

...the patient has written a complaint letter to the police exposing her husband's abuse towards her...she insists that Dr. K must read her letter...she wants her statement to be audio recorded too...

...during the telephone conversation with her husband, she became nervous and agitated...

...she received a visit from two of her daughters; she was very happy about that...

...the patient spends most of her time in her room, very pensive. When asked if she is fine, she answers, everything is OK. She is sad that her family does not come to visit her...

...she is convinced that she will be leaving and so, explains to us that she doesn't need to create social relations to other patients...

...the husband has refused to take her home...the patient is very sad and says that her husband is a liar...

...today the interview was conducted with the patient's brother and his wife. According to them, the husband is violent.

*...he mentioned that the husband has been **sexually abusing minors** (?)...in the presence of his wife....*

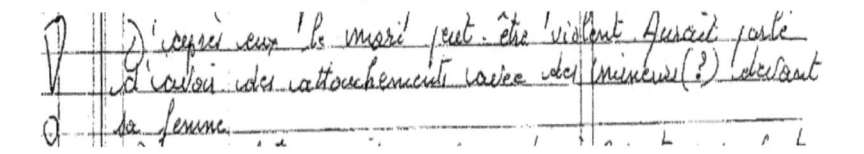

...the patient's brother says that she became sick around 1991 (according to the husband, his wife became sick in her twenties!!) ...

...the patient tells us that she wants to go home, despite her husband hitting her...she says that she has no energy to take care of the household on her own...she can't imagine living without her husband and she can't imagine having a new partner...she is scared to lose contact with her children...she feels very alone...

...she feels very bored here...she does not feel needed... she says that apart from playing ping-pong all day, she does not do anything...she says she does not belong here...

...the patient says that she is more than fed up with being here. It has been too many months already...she says that if her husband refuses to pick her up, then her brother can come and if he refuses, then she can ask for a divorce immediately and get out of here once and for all.

...she says that her heart is torn each time she needs to leave her children after she's allowed to go home for the weekend...

...the patient is relaxed and smiley today...she says she feels better and better.... she says she is looking forward to her next weekend home in a few weeks' time...

...she has gone out with her fellow patients and bought sweets, which she shared between the other patients upon her return...

...she wants to tell us that her 5 euros for the cafeteria are slowly running out

...the patient feels rejected and incapacitated. She has lost all reflexes to take initiatives and to think for herself...she has abandoned every responsibility for herself and others...

...she says she wants to go to Church and pray, however, she does not feel that this hospital allows her to practice her Christianity...

.... the patient seems very passive, except when she talks about her six children, she becomes emotional...

...she feels that her husband has created this diagnosis and is keeping her silent with medication...she also says that she is not angry with him for what he has done to her; she forgives him...

...the patient, despite being highly educated as a gynecologist, feels like she has no resources left to stand for herself. She refuses to do anything positive for herself, as if she is punishing herself. Why? Because of whom?

...because of the strict rules imposed by her husband,

the patient is kept out of the kitchen and does not participate in the daily family life...

...this patient is a prisoner in her own home...

...this patient has given up, needs to be stimulated for the most basic activities...

...the patient is excessively dependent on her husband... she believes she can't survive without him...she needs to be given the confidence to use her own resources again; away from her husband...

...the patient feels very alone in Luxembourg...

...Visit from the ambulatory medical team to administer the injection at home in the presence of her husband... AS USUAL, her husband always replies on behalf of his wife...

...after speaking with other medical staff, the consensus is that the patient's husband wants to keep his wife passive and unable to care for herself. He seems to not want his wife to get better...but why? What is he scared of?

...her husband is very complicated...but we can't speak to his wife when she is home, as apparently, she is not allowed to use the phone!!!...

...he has become more and more difficult; his wife does not trust anyone who enters the house, including us...

...the patient seems to be fully submissive to her husband...I can never talk to the patient alone; her

husband is omnipresent and answers for her...

...the husband finds every excuse in the world for his wife to stay locked up at home...

...we can't do our job properly, the husband does not let us come close to his wife, everything is done in the corridor in five minutes...

...we are not allowed to speak to the patient or any other member of the family...

...the patient is fully dependent on her husband and does not have her own money...

...today, the patient herself asked to be given the injection, we are really wondering – WHY? Is it her way of staying locked up in her bubble...to be disconnected? Is it her only way of enduring this painful reality?

...the patient is not at all comfortable in the presence of her husband...

...she is much more relaxed when we meet her alone... but still often meets the nurses in the corridor with her bottle of water, to quickly swallow her pills and get it over with...

....to all appearances, she is still sequestrated...she does not take any initiative without her husband's approval...

...suspicion of extreme abuse by her husband...please pay close attention...regular visits to the patient's home...patient feels unbearable psychological pain...

please hospitalise her away from her abuser in case of clear complaints by the patient.

Chapter Five

His Mask

So, what is known about Nicolas' childhood and upbringing? I've heard it time and time again that sexual abusers are often past victims themselves. This may be an explanation but never an excuse for traumatising new victims. Nicolas was born into a family of 11 children. He has four brothers and six sisters. He's a son of a businessman and a housewife. Despite being a household of 13 people, the family was well off and did not seem to struggle. The parents could comfortably offer their children a pleasant childhood. Born in the 1950s, his first years of life were, let's say peculiar.

Back then, obviously born as a male child, his mother did not want people to 'curse' him as apparently 'jealous eyes' would envy her for giving birth to the more precious gender. His mother therefore told everyone that her child was a girl. When it was time to register Nicolas' birth at the town hall, a relative unknowingly recorded the new-born as a female child called Nicole. This mistake didn't come to light until Nicolas was six years old and about to start primary school. The gender on the birth certificate just didn't match the gender of the child about to be schooled and he was refused entry.

In despair, Nicolas' parents and six-year-old Nicolas were summoned to court to clear up the misunderstanding. During the hearing, the only way of setting the records straight was for Nicolas to pull down his trousers to finally prove once and for all that he was a boy and not a girl. This scene was very humiliating for little Nicolas. He could not understand that he had been a girl for six years, while actually being a boy. Who knows, perhaps this incident subconsciously messed up little Nicolas so that he had to 'prove' himself over and over again as a boy, and later on as a man. He may have needed to show his masculinity after this trauma. We will never know.

To make things worse, he was given a new name after being known by another name for six years. Despite being 'Nicole' on the birth certificate, he was known at home as 'Marc'. During the court hearing, the judge told his parents that he can't accept 'Marc' as the new name. It had to be a variant of Nicole as that was the original name. His parents then turned 'Nicole' into 'Nicolas' and so the confusion began for young Nicolas. One can only imagine that this incident may have traumatised Nicolas to the point of causing sexual deviations, who knows.

From what I have known all these years, Nicolas was a shy, obedient, and kind character. He even rocked the perfect student look with his hair parting. He was always up for making parallels between Bible verses and real-life situations. The perfect groom for any girl, looking to marry. He was a committed Church servant and growing up, he would hold the Sunday school and Bible study at Church. He was set to become a monk and dedicate his life and celibacy to Jesus and God. Life, however, had other plans for him. The accidental wedding with Nelly in 1980 changed his destiny. In hindsight, it would have been preferable, he followed his heart and God by hibernating for good in the Sahara Desert.

Nicolas grew up in a close-knit God-loving family. He loved his father dearly and has always spoken highly of him. I have never met my grandfather, he died shortly after Nicolas' wedding. Nicolas always portrayed his father as the impersonation of the perfect parent though he was seemingly mostly absent on business trips. Neither of his parents seemed to be of the 'dominant' type and so, one can't necessarily explain a 'violent' environment causing Nicolas to become a wife-beating child molester. There must have been other factors playing a role in his ethics taking a sick turn.

Later during the trial, it was mentioned that Nicolas himself was sexually assaulted as a teen during a Scout's camp. Again, this incident may be an explanation, but not an excuse. Nicolas was the type of child who would not draw attention to himself. He was definitely an introvert. He acted beyond his age and therefore felt misunderstood by his peers. He chose to study pharmacy and moved to Dubai straight after his studies. He eagerly built a hospital there with a group of British nuns, with whom he quickly developed a great affinity. His ten siblings went on to become highly educated professionals spread all over the world, some of them quite renowned.

Nicolas was a master in disguise. One could never predict his mood. He had his family on hyper-vigilant standby with his ever-changing temper. He would go from smiley to evil in no time. He was a ticking time bomb and there was no way of sensing his outbursts. One day, coming back from a Scouts camp, I can't remember what exactly our 'misdemeanour' was, but he ended up burning all our uniforms, he was in rage. When he was angry at us, mostly Andreas, my mother and I got the full-blown fury. The other four children seemed to have been spared by his physical violence, I am not sure why. Common punishments included burning our bare skin with cutlery well warmed up in an open flame, hitting us until blood was flowing or force us to stay outside in the cold weather without shoes or jacket. Regardless of age, involvement or gravity of the wrongdoings, the same sanctions were applicable. He seemed to sadistically enjoy seeing others suffer, perhaps even more, if he was the perpetrator.

He always chose to appear poor, despite being wealthy and kept up that image over the years. He wore old clothes, barely changing them and was always walking around with that worn out jacket, carrying that infamous bundle of keys. He could be heard walking from metres away. He casually installed a very fancy sauna and jacuzzi in the veranda, both of which became crime scenes later. He could not have been that poor then, could he? When did it all go wrong? How did a supposedly good Christian turn into a child molester? How did this dedicated Church servant become a perverted wife-beating monster? There is no doubt that Nicolas perfectly matches the profile of a narcissistic pervert. Not surprisingly, he was drawn to an easy prey, my mother. The sweet, gentle, insecure empath.

He would charm any stranger with his broad knowledge of pretty much everything. Of course, always relating his speech to Jesus Christ to support his sayings. Despite being an introvert as a child, he seemed to have become more and more outgoing as the years went on. He was receiving compliments, admiration and most of all pity, a very crucial element to feed his ego.

Despite all the cruelties, that Nicolas was making his wife and eldest daughter endure at home, day, and night, he was always regarded as the sacrificing, good, caring father and husband. How utterly incredible with the crimes that we know had been happening within the four walls over decades. He was effortlessly keeping up his mask for the world to see and hail him as the hero that his wife and children were just so lucky to have. He used to sit in his armchair with the six children on the floor in front of him. He would read out of the Holy Bible and relate the verses to real life. He portrayed himself as the ultimate wise Christian.

He was making sure that we become decent members of society, what a hypocrite. He became the impersonation of the Messiah. He was God's son, sent to Earth to save humanity. After his arrest, this was his only explanation to his family as to why he was in prison. It was his mission to put the criminals on the right path. My siblings never doubted for a second that this man was Heaven sent. Early on during the investigations, Denise told the police that she would die for him; didn't they know WHO they are unfairly holding in jail?

Nicolas was adamant to keep his wife chronically 'sick'. On the one hand, to be able to be praised as the 'saviour' in the eyes of his surrounding and on the other hand, to be able to freely abuse his daughter without the interference of my mother. She had to be silenced, no matter the price to pay. He was the loving father and husband, who was doing everything to keep his large family intact despite his wife's 'sickness'. I regret that child protection service was not alerted at any point. Who knows, perhaps a competent social worker could have seen the truth behind his mask.

Being a pharmacist, he had full knowledge of the medication, that his wife was under against her will. After arriving in Luxembourg from the UK in the 1980s, he quit his profession to pursue that of a businessman. His activities couldn't have been more diverse. From iron steel, stamps, fruit and vegetables over to wood, his palette was limitless. Starting in the 1990's, he used me as his personal secretary. I was just starting secondary school and had to type his business letters, often until late at night, regardless of it being a weekday or not. He would visit later at night regardless.

My insomnia was getting worse since the nightly visits started at 9 years old. My secretary job debuted when Nicolas got hold of a very old computer. We are talking floppy disc era. I would sign his letters with 'managing director', whatever that meant at the time. I had no idea what I was typing, who I was typing to and what the trades were about. I obeyed as the good girl, the favourite daughter. Nicolas was giving me responsibilities beyond my maturity and made me grow up too fast.

Nicolas' philatelic career started around 1995 when he was working as a kitchen assistant in a nursing home in Luxembourg city. One must say that Nicolas always had an affinity for the elderly population. Perhaps for his own gain, perhaps hoping and wishing that one of these days, he'd hit the jackpot and gets mentioned in a will? One wealthy Luxembourgish woman comes to mind. Nicolas entertained a relationship with her. She was about 90 years old, and he must have been 45. He would buy her groceries, visit her regularly in her luxury apartment and buy her favourite pastry, an 'eclair au chocolat'. He used to tell me back then that he also satisfied this woman, along with many others, sexually. Nicolas had no limits as to what information he would share with me, whether it was age appropriate or not. He had no ethics.

Stamp collectors are often ridiculed but once one knows how lucrative this philately business can be, it doesn't feel as ridiculous anymore. Very old stamps, in complete sheets, as they came from the factory are priceless. Discovering this niche, Nicolas didn't hesitate to buy random collections from elderly people, who obviously had no idea of the value of their stamps. He often found his preys in a weekly paper called *Lux Bazar*. As children, we would go with him to these people and sit with him as he screened the albums, picking up the stamps with his special tweezers and inspecting them in detail with his magnifying glass in the hope of spotting highly valued stamps. He would then offer the sellers a buying price, that was a tiny percentage of the actual market value of these stamps, making the people think they made a good deal. Unbeknownst to them, Nicolas was going to sell their stamps and multiply his profit based on their ignorance.

Slowly, Nicolas got to know the main actors in the philately market and created strong connections. Our house became a negotiating bazar, where random people, mostly old white men would turn up to view stamps and the negotiation would begin. Sometimes, the discussion would end in a big argument between buyer and seller and the visitor would storm out in disagreement. As children, we would have to go with Nicolas to the Sunday morning stamp market in Luxembourg town, in a posh area called Belair. The weekly market was held in a cultural centre. Each seller would have a table, with their goods nicely presented.

Beside old stamps, one could also make good trades with old postcards, old coins, and other artefacts from all over the world. We were Nicolas' little helpers, who would help him with the boxes. I despised that weekly trip from the beginning. I hated going there as a child and having to converse with these men. Nicolas had a way of attracting sleazy men, who would think it's appropriate to seductively speak to a child as if they were talking to an adult. Nicolas had no objection to old men flirting with his young daughters. For the children, the fun part of the Sunday trip was the *McDonald's* lunch that followed, but only if Nicolas made enough profit that morning.

Slowly, the house became more and more filled with boxes of stamps. My mother hated her husband's new business, she had had enough of the clutter. At some point, there was no room anymore, so Nicolas transformed the full upper floor into a stamp dump. He would go to markets all over the world and trade, mostly tax-free. Based on the ignorance of the general population about stamps and their true market value, most deals were done under the table.

As opposed to other artefacts, the stamp market has its own price guide, which is reissued each year. In Luxembourg, for example, the main catalogue is called *Prifix*, in which the value of each stamp ever issued is stated. Of course, new stamps, fresh out of the factory, that have never been stuck in an album principally have a higher value than those that are hinged. The third price category is the used stamp, that was found on an envelope or postcard. Despite, being a fascinating hobby, that I also loved spending my time with when it was not imposed, I do have an aversion to anything related to stamps today.

Nicolas started a 'friendship' with an elderly man called Mr. B in the nursing home he was working at. He would visit him regularly and made sure he was feeling well cared of. This aged man was holding the biggest and most precious stamp collection in Luxembourg. He had tons of complete sheets of rare Luxembourgish stamps, still fresh out of the factory. Following the death of Mr. B, Nicolas made sure to hold the full monopoly in purchasing these stamps for a fraction of the market value, thereby making profit after profit. Nicolas had a way of finding the highest bidders for the stamps and he didn't mind travelling thousands of miles, if it meant he would get to make a good deal. Pulling his rolling suitcase across airports, nobody would ever suspect that it contained complete sheets and rare stamps worth a fortune.

Step by step, Nicolas bought the biggest collection of stamps in Luxembourg from Mr B's children. This trade was a game-changer for him as slowly he was known to be holding the largest and most important stock of stamps in Luxembourg and thereby attracted the interest of local buyers, some prepared to pay anything for a rare stamp. As children, we would spend hours detaching the stamps that were stuck on letters and postcards by immersing them in water, sorting them by country, stamp date and series and arranging them into albums using tweezers. We were an integral part of the family business, only we only felt like free child labour.

As the business grew and me being the child secretary, I had to create hundreds of invoices, many of them false as ordered by my 'managing director'. He would dictate ad hoc figures that I would have to insert in the *Word* invoice template. I had absolutely no clue what I was doing. I didn't know why he dictated made up numbers without an actual transaction occurring. A couple of years later, I randomly saw on the news that there was a Razzia in Spain in a collectibles company. I had travelled with Nicolas to Madrid to visit that company before. The news was talking about a scandal, a Ponzi fraud scheme. I had no idea what that meant.

The name of the company rang a bell as it was one of those, that I was made to issue invoices to. My genitor panicked when he saw the news and somehow from that moment on, I never wrote a single invoice. Until today, I have no idea what his involvement was, but I am set to find out to complete my puzzle. Since being on a quest, digging up the past, I might as well, dig up everything. Perhaps, I can make him return to prison as he's still out on probation, I wish nothing more than that.

In the 1990's, through another stamp collector, Nicolas landed a deal in the iron steel industry in Luxembourg. He was able to sell a high furnace to a third world country and thereby cash in on a big profit during this affair. I was typing letters between buyer and seller, communicating about millions of Luxembourgish Francs. I was totally out of sync with my peers at school, who merely had a crush on Jon Bon Jovi or Kurt Cobain and were enjoying a carefree childhood and adolescence.

Another out of scope business was Nicolas' trades with Papua New Guinea. He used to regularly travel there, and he was hailed as the Good Samaritan. He used to buy toys from Singapore for the local children on the island and he was adopted by the locals as one of their own. He started trading in timber and when he returned to Luxembourg, he would be proudly showing us the photos of him in traditional clothing, making sure to point out his local topless female acquaintances along with a 'funny' anecdote. Nicolas would be travelling all around the world and nobody would exactly know what his 'businesses' consisted of.

All we remember as children, is that he was always the first one to bring back the latest technology gadgets. As such, early in the 1990's, Nicolas bought a videophone on one of his Japan trips. He dealt in them as well. God knows what this man hasn't traded in. It was revolutionary back then, to be able to see the other person on a small screen attached to the phone. It was videoconferencing twenty years in advance, long before the invention of the internet.

Another one of his favourite gizmos, was a 'toilet shower'. It was a Japanese toilet seat, equipped with everything one can imagine. The automatic washing, drying and perfuming following the deed made the toilet visit ever so long. With an 8-person household, one can imagine, that this technological addition wasn't as welcomed as Nicolas had hoped. Sometimes, the apparatus would go out of control and douche everywhere except the spots where it was supposed to. So, often, we left the WC with soaked clothes and a washed face. The multiple buttons on the controller were too sophisticated and it may have been best to stick with the old-fashioned way.

Nicolas always made sure his image was sound. Perhaps, that worked for my siblings and his surrounding, who could not see his true face behind his mask, but for my mother and myself, he's always been a disgusting man. Our image of him was real and not falsified. He could not fool us, despite pretending to be a caring and loving father and husband. My mother and I repeatedly saw what he was capable of. All we could do was tolerate his cruelties in order to survive.

Feeling body conscious, he regularly went on diets and pretty much stopped eating. He would only drink innumerable cups of coffee throughout the day. Because of the fasting, he would have bad breath. It was very nauseating to be sitting near him, let alone being forced to kiss him. The weeks of fasting would be followed by sugar cravings, making him ingest large amounts of *Snickers* chocolate bars. Wearing his unwashed clothes and his heavy sweat-filled jacket, one can imagine the smelly breeze that always followed him. He used to spend hours in the sauna at home, in the hope of losing weight and was always showing off his results on high technology scales.

Surprisingly, being foreign himself, he was one of the biggest racists I had encountered in my life. He used to tell us that we must marry a white Luxembourger and there was no tolerance for any other nationality. During his late adolescence, Andreas got into a relationship with a dark-skinned girl from the Bahamas. I can only assume that this encounter was made possible through the advances of the world wide web, that was very novel back then. He went over to visit her and they were planning a common future together.

Nicolas, from the beginning, was against that relationship. Not because of the long distance but merely because the girl was neither Luxembourgish nor white. Marrying a dark-skinned Luxembourger was not going to cut it either, it had to be a WHITE Luxembourger. After heated arguments between father and son, Andreas saw himself breaking up with his girlfriend. He was already at the age of taking his own decisions and yet, he was still under the absolute dominance of our guru. Years later, when Nicolas was locked up in prison, Andreas sent him an enthusiastic, heartfelt letter to announce to him that he will finally be so proud of him, as he has met a white Luxembourgish girl, *just like he always wanted*. Andreas said he couldn't wait to introduce her to him! He was about 30 years old at the time.

During my first year at university, a dark-skinned student Edward fancied me. When Nicolas received a diverted text message from that young man to his phone, revealing his crush on me, he did not hesitate to call him personally. He carried on stating that 'Mary would never date a black man; how could he even believe that he had a chance with her. Mary was too good for him, the only person she would be dating would be from a pure white Luxembourgish family'. I listened to all of this in embarrassment from afar and needless to say that Edward despised me after that racist phone call.

The running statement of Nicolas regarding his order for a white Luxembourgish life partner was 'I did not come to Luxembourg for my children to bring us back to black, I want future generations to whiten and not to darken'. Strangely, I ended up marrying a white Luxembourger, was it unconsciously driven by our racist upbringing? I will never know. It's true that I was more inclined that way, without consciously thinking about it.

Not only was he the biggest racist, but he would be categorising people according to their birth month. This went beyond astrology. I doubt he even knew about the different star signs. Whenever he met a new person, the first question would be 'when were you born'? After that, he would either treat them as smart, naive, stupid, or magical. It goes without saying that his birth month, September, was simultaneously of the smart and magical type. People born in that month were, to him THE BEST people. Denise was always praised as smart, and he considered her to be his mini me. She was born one day after his birthday. He never punished her. She was always 'Miss Perfect' in our family.

On the other hand, people born in May and June were to be considered 'naive and stupid'. My mother was born in May, and I was born in June. We were put in the same 'stupid' pot very early on. Strangely, we grew up believing this system, I mean he was the father, the only authority that we had. If he says that people born in November are stupid, then they are, right? According to my abuser's theory, people born in November share the same 'naïve and stupid' gene as people born in May and June. My mother and I were regarded as the 'same' and my siblings always considered me as 'sick' as my mother; they have ever since our childhood. The only sick person with all this evidence on the table, is Nicolas - a perverted magical manipulator.

I have often felt like the little girl in *Matilda* by Roald Dahl. I always felt totally misplaced in this family. I constantly lived in my head to escape and not go crazy. School was my safe place, only I had no Miss Honey to confide in. Growing up, my father often told me that I was swapped at the maternity hospital in

Dubai. My skin was indeed darker than that of my parents and siblings and therefore his theory started to make sense to me. I so hoped it was true. I wished my real parents were still out there and we would be reunited one day, once I escaped that hell. As a child, I often created my perfect parents in my mind.

The couple was made up of a French children's programme presenter called Dorothée married to Angus MacGyver. I so wanted them to be my parents. Never did it cross my mind, that physically they didn't resemble me or that they lived on different continents. It was not realistic and yet, it worked to keep me daydreaming, wishing and hoping that it could work out one day. It felt that I was the only one, besides my mother, who really knew who 'perfect' Nicolas really was. She had long lost respect for her husband and couldn't even address him by his name. She used to 'shhhhh' him, even in public. She did not see him as a decent human being anymore that deserved to be called by his name. For my mother and I, his mask had fallen a long time ago; that moment he crossed an unimaginable ethical barrier.

Chapter Six

His Cruelty

Nicolas was cruel. There are nearly no words in the vocabulary to describe how heartless this man was. I thought dedicating a full chapter to his wrongdoings was logical, but I realise that the gravity of his actions will never be truly felt through the lines. He had no drop of empathy for his victims. It's as if with each vile act he got away with, he felt more and more confident to turn up the level a bit further, and some more. Nobody was interfering after all, so it can't have been that bad. Besides, for a narcissistic pervert, the notion of guilt is non-existent and whatever he does is rightful and can be justified in his immature mind.

I have a hard time finding any justification for his crimes. How does a father and husband get this last push to cross the ethical barrier from one day to the other? From all the evidence I have, I am beyond convinced that my mother never wanted children to start with. It would not surprise me if Nicolas raped her at least six times to impregnate her. Let's remind ourselves that she was a highly educated woman, a gynaecologist obstetrician even. So, if one person could have known how NOT to get pregnant, it was surely her, wasn't it? If Nicolas was able to cross the barrier of sexually abusing his daughter for over 16 years, nobody needs to make me believe that he respected his wife to the point of checking for consent first prior to sexual intercourse.

As children, we were brainwashed by him to believe that our mother had abandoned us, that she was sick, that she was a danger to us, that we should treat her like a threat, a child, an inconvenience. He made us sign letters, lie to the psychiatrists, treat her like a burden. We were all embarrassed of her, she was dead and alive at the same time. She used to experience the full panoply of the antipsychotic drug-induced extrapyramidal Parkinson's disease resembling side-effects. These included slow pace, tremor, restlessness, involuntary muscle contractions, just to name a few. Nicolas got us convinced that she was the 'bad' parent. It's like we had this mother at home, but we needed to 'hide' her from the outside world. We all had this dark secret for over decades, and we couldn't really talk about it. It's like we could not expose what was going on at home and we had to play a role outside to keep up the 'happy family' image imposed by our guru. I lived in constant fear and never even thought of telling anyone about the abuse. It's like I very well integrated the fact that my future will be the same as my mother's if this 'secret' ever came out. I fully convinced myself that Nicolas had the ultimate power over me, as I had repeatedly witnessed how easy it was for him to break another human being, with no shame or remorse.

What would people say, if they found out that our father was torturing our mother in front of us? What would people say, if they knew that we had digital codes on the kitchen door so that our mother would not enter the kitchen and cook? What would people say, if they knew that our mother was sitting on the sofa all day, looking dead, silenced with heavy medication to not be a disturbance to our almighty father, who was freely abusing his daughter, all this happening with a perverted consensus in that family?

He made us think that he was the 'good' parent, that he sacrificed everything for his children. My five siblings and I grew up believing his lies. In that sense, we are all victims of his actions, all six of us but seemingly only I had the mental strength to see through it and not take everything at face value.

Until today, Nicolas shows off at every opportunity to remind everyone that thanks to him, his children have become educated despite all the hardships. Funnily, that man brags about me as his daughter and my success in life being his sole merit. The audacity and lack of self-reflection is truly shocking.

Beside the physical punishments in the basement, with his bare hands or the use of a ruler or any other utensil he could get hold of, the psychological abuse was omnipresent in our lives. Back then in Remich, when we were young, he would always threaten to take and leave us outside the house fully naked if we misbehaved. The psychological abuse, however, was more subtle. The manipulation, the lies, the guilt-tripping, the gaslighting, the intimidation, the humiliation, the criticism, and the incapacitation every day, were integral elements in our upbringing. The constant feeling of owing our father for simply 'existing' has remained up to this day with my five other siblings. They just can't detach from him, which for me, is very difficult to understand. Perhaps his death, will finally release them from his shackles?

When I was nine years old, my father first molested me. My mother was not home; she had just been taken to the hospital, leaving me in the hands of my criminal. Up until that day, I had never felt any different to my siblings. Slowly, my father made me his favourite, subtly isolating me from the crowd and feeding into my siblings' ever-growing jealousy towards me.

Over the years that followed, I remained awake, fearing the nightly visits. I dreaded the creaking of the wooden stairs and my bedroom door squeaking while slowly being opened. I would go to school with little sleep, if any at all, and still be able to function and score high grades. My internal system seemed to radically accommodate what was happening to me for me to cope and to unconsciously carry on as normal. This abuse went on for SIXTEEN long and painful years behind closed doors in harrowing silence. When the abuse first happened, I was sharing a bedroom with three of my siblings. That did not worry Nicolas.

Later, I shared a room with only one sibling before I had my own room. I remember that my room was adjacent to Denise's room, only separated with a door behind which was my bed. When Nicolas would visit me on a nightly basis, I would kick that door with my foot to make noise in the hope that someone would wake up and interrupt the abuse. Nicolas would tell me to stop as I may be waking someone up with my noise. He used to tightly hold my foot to prevent me from kicking that door. Where were the other 6 people in the house while I was helplessly succumbing day and night for years to this disgusting man? I felt disgusted, dirty, ashamed, and lived in constant, absolute fear of my own father in my own home. I absolutely hated my childhood, adolescence, and young adulthood.

If this is hell, then I was certainly in the middle of it and there was no way out. I was trapped and this man had the ultimate power over me. He was obsessed with my being, partly for his own pleasure and partly, which I can only imagine was fear of me speaking out. I can't imagine that he was not scared of his dirty secret coming out one day and him being in huge trouble. Throughout all those years, he smartly made me believe all these years that if 'our' secret comes out, I will be the one punished and not him. I will be the one sent to prison. He had often threatened to send me to a youth shelter if I didn't conform. I had, of course, seen how easy it was for him to repeatedly get rid of my mother with one simple telephone call.

I had no other choice than to believe what he was saying was true. He was the adult after all, and I had nobody else to tell me that the opposite was true. He made sure I remained ignorant. Whenever I read about 'sexual abuse' in my teen magazine; for my own survival, I always justified to myself that I was not concerned. I convinced myself that sexual abuse is always linked to violence and what my own father was doing was 'medical' after all and in no way sexual. I don't know what it is like to enjoy carefree years with unconditional care and love from parents. I have never had a chance to experience that pure love that I am fortunate enough to give to my own children today.

Over the years, I had perfected my smile behind which was hiding a painful double life. I was closely being watched in order not to raise any suspicions about the abuse. What would have happened if I had not pretended everything was fine? I dare not imagine. There were plenty of silent cries for help and hints of the abuse, but nobody spoke openly or took any action, neither within nor outside the family. Nicolas was a charismatic Christian figure who compared himself to God. He was respected and admired for his apparent generosity and kindness. Appearances can be deceptive.

Out of the six children, I would often travel around the world with Nicolas on his business trips. I would go to far away places with him including Tokyo, Hong Kong, Macau, Singapore, Toronto, Los Angeles and

Dubai. He always made sure that we receive one double bed and not two single beds when asked at the hotel reception, to the surprise of the employee since I was already a teenager and later, a young adult. I often felt like the hotel reception employees must have thought that I was not his daughter but some sort of escort/prostitute that he rented out for his pleasure. He often made me watch pornographic movies with him in the hotel room. I was fully at his mercy, far away from my home although even in my own home I never felt safe.

I was made out to be the special one and I would receive presents while the other five siblings would be dismissed and disadvantaged. They usually received my old belongings that I no longer used. This open favouritism by Nicolas towards me only produced feelings of guilt and shame in me – they were my brothers and sisters and nothing about the situation felt right nor made any sense. It only separated me further. All I was craving at the time was a connection to my siblings and to feel loved and safe as any child would.

I was treated like a princess and always placed on a pedestal by Nicolas for being the good obedient student and his pretty daughter that he loved to show off. The healthy boundaries between a father and daughter were completely destroyed. Nicolas' behaviour indirectly enraged and created jealousy among my siblings from an early age, quite understandably so – who would not object to this special treatment to one child and not the others? At primary and later in secondary school, the other children would envy me and 'wish they were me' as they saw how well travelled I was continuously spoiled by a multitude of lavish gifts. In my head, I wish I could have told them that I was imprisoned and so desperately unhappy. If only they knew of the dark truth, they would not have felt this way towards me.

My mother always defended herself all as she could when she was being tortured by her husband. She once pulled his testicles in self-defence, which I was very pleased about to say the least, not only to witness her standing up for herself but for him to experience some of his own treatment in return. I have a vivid memory of being on a family trip on the Belgian Coast. I must have been about eight as Mira was still a baby at the time. In the hotel room, Nicolas ordered Nelly to change Mira's diapers, to which she replied that he should do it. He quickly lost his temper and while changing Mira, he scooped up her stools out of her sodden diaper and stuffed them in my mother's mouth by force. As if that was not humiliating enough, he proceeded to wickedly hitting her with a keyring that held a bunch of keys on her thighs until she was black and blue and howling and whimpering in pain.

Life continued and so did the nightly abuse. The survival instinct was in full action and no matter how much I defended myself, I had absolutely no chance against an adult. With each questioning, my father would age appropriately justify his actions to me by saying it's educational, medical or plain normal. I was very confused. Did my father love me? Was I really special? Did he just use me? How did he justify this abuse in his head for him to feel like it was righteous? How could he love me if he was doing me wrong at the same time? Why did I need to be the special one? How I wished to be another sister who could sleep through the night. How I wished to not be scared every single night. I developed hatred for this man while everyone else loved him. I knew his real face and I had to keep quiet and keep on smiling. Despite me slapping and scratching him to defend myself, he was always stronger than me.

When I reached the age of fourteen, I had lost ten kilograms within a short space of time, yet nobody seemed to be bothered or notice this cry for help. I felt invisible to the world and the people in it. Consciously or unconsciously, I did not want to have any of the feminine assets that puberty brought to me. My period stopped, my breasts disappeared, and I was surviving on just one slice of bread a day. The physical, sexual and psychological abuse continued, and nobody was alarmed about what was going on, not the teachers nor the family. No one seemed to spot any signs of distress within me, and I didn't dare to speak out. I was left alone to succumb to the suffering that this disgusting man enforced onto me each day. Nobody wondered or questioned as to why he would wake up in the morning in my bed; his daughter's bed. Nobody thought twice, it became just the normal routine. All quite unbelievable to consider that this could actually happen within a family.

The years passed, the abuse continued, and I was living a horrid double life. During the day, I was functioning on very little sleep. The adrenaline chugging throughout my body must have kept me wired in survival mode. I was fitting in with my peers. I had Backstreet Boys posters on my walls, fancied B-Rok and consistently bought a German teen magazine called *Bravo* every Thursday for 52 Luxembourgish Francs. I was an overachiever, scoring high grades and smiling on the outside. I convincingly wore my mask that hid my pain all too well. Then I became terrified at night of that horrible and sickening man coming into my room.

Sexual predators are rarely people outside of the child's circle of trust. They sugar coat the abuse during the years that they act on their depraved desires, conditioning their victim from a young age that this is what fathers, or whoever they may be, do. As I matured and became more aware, I was able to realise more and more that the abuse was not 'normal', yet I never told anyone for 16 years out of the most profound fear and shame that gnawed into my psyche. Still, however, I continually pushed it away, in order to maintain the secret. Had I spoken out, the potential consequences of what may happen to me then, felt too much for me to even comprehend.

I had seen how my father was capable of imprisoning my mother for months at a time in a psychiatric hospital. She had no voice. It was the precise projection of what may happen to me if I had gone against someone like him. What if it made everything much worse? How would I deal with that? I could clearly imagine the fury of my father, as I pictured his angry face in my mind and heard the wrath in his voice. And who would believe me, against his words? What if I somehow found the courage to tell somebody and they didn't believe what I said? There was also the strange feeling that I would be betraying my father and how could I do that? It was easier and better that I kept quiet. It somehow must be my fault after all, I convinced myself.

Since the early days of the abuse, I used to ask Nicolas why he touched me and not the other sisters. His replies were always the same; that the other sisters did not 'need' that. I was, according to him, the shy and ugly one out of his four daughters and that I needed to 'get out of myself'. According to him, the other three were open minded girls and I was 'special' and different. He used to say that they were comfortable with their bodies while I always hid my chest with my long hair because I was extremely timid. How could I ever be comfortable with the body that he misused for his own pleasure? This man broke my self-esteem before it even had a chance to develop in a healthy way. I apparently needed more 'help'. Many years later, Nicolas' defence during the criminal trial was that, out of all of his children, I was the only one to have inherited my mother's 'mental illness' and that is why I obviously needed more attention. The judges did not fall for that.

As the secret should remain between us, my father told me that 'others wouldn't understand'. To help me cope, as although I pushed a lot of my feelings down, they were always emerging to haunt me, I started looking for foundations with the aim of cleansing myself. Very early on, I prayed daily, and I would go to church on my own and confess for what I had done with this strong belief that I was the culprit. It felt like my church visits gave me the clean consciousness that I needed to survive. It seemed that by going every week, the abuse was erased, albeit temporarily. Week after week, this warped cycle continued. I felt very dirty as if I had done something wrong. I was forgiven each week. How could the world of a little girl become so distorted by the actions of a deranged man? I felt quite out of place in church. Apart from me, there was always a Portuguese neighbour who kneeled on the floor and a few other older people. The only other young people that I would see on a weekly basis would be the few that were forced to go by their parents and the acolytes.

The abuse was neatly and conveniently packaged and presented to me as presents, care and love. It was always age appropriately justified as a 'learning experience' in order to 'know how to treat men later' or 'that all fathers do that'. I could not understand how an authority figure who is supposed to love and protect could do this much disgusting harm to their child. I experienced many feelings of conflict, as parts of me felt it was wrong but parts of me believed it was justified because Nicolas is a caring parent after all. I continued to function and score the best grades on very little sleep that enabled me to survive.

I keenly moved to the UK for my studies and hoped that the physical distance would stop the abuse, but Nicolas followed me there. He hired a private detective to track my every move and monitor every person that I was in contact with. These people were then thoroughly investigated and threatened away. During the trial, he stupidly handed in documents as 'evidence', that he couldn't possibly have access to, unless he had hacked my email accounts. Unbeknownst to me, my phone calls and messages were diverted to his phone. He had free access to my email accounts, with the help of his hacker son, Leonard. Nicolas was obsessed with my person and no-one else was allowed access to me. I was his possession and if I did not do as I was told, he would threaten me in the most horrible ways.

Many years had passed by then, the conditioning of that little girl was still working on her as a young adult, and he had gained full control. On the outside, I appeared to be an independent, smiley, educated, fully functioning healthcare professional. The reality behind the mask was very different. This deranged man had full control of my every move and the people I was in contact with – he was running the show.

Over the years, my father's threats became more and more intense, and I would fear for my life. Nicolas was two faced and his façade continued, never slipping.

On the outside, he was a caring father and a generous Christian, yet only I knew his other dark disgusting side, but I couldn't share it with anyone. I grew up with so much disgust towards this man. I was alone with it, for years, that little girl was left to fight on her own, every single night. No matter how much resistance I would give him, he remained stronger physically and psychologically and had full control. I was entirely at his mercy, and nobody could help me. They didn't even know for goodness' sake. That's how tragic and pathetic it was.

Nicolas even found new coercive methods to control and abuse me as an adult. Despite being a highly educated professional, Nicolas would force me to transfer all my salary to his account so that I would have very little money left, and just enough to fill my tank so that I could drive to work every day. He made me financially dependent on him with my own money. He diverted all my calls and messages to his phone and was aware of my every move and communications either by stalking me physically or through the information the detective would provide him with. He often showed up in the UK with no warning and threatened people that I was in contact with to leave me alone or he would harm their reputation in one way or another. I always made sure to save any boy's name under an invented girl's name in my phone, even at the age of 26.

At the end of this chapter, you'll see an elephant. This big, strong elephant is held by a fragile rope at its back foot. The elephant could easily break free, but it doesn't. Why not?

As a man was passing by, he suddenly stopped, and he was confused. There were no chains, and the elephant was not kept in a locked cage. The man went up to a trainer close by and asked him why the elephant didn't even try to break free, when it so easily could. The trainer replied: 'When it was very young and much smaller, we use the same size rope to tie the back foot, and at that age, it's enough to restrain the animal. As it grows up, it is conditioned to believe that it can't break free. It remains in the belief that the rope can still hold it, so it never even tries to escape.'

Like the man passing by, wondering why this elephant did not set itself free with one simple step, many people have asked me why, did I not press charges when I was younger when I must have realised that the abuse was not 'normal' in any way. Like the elephant, I had also been conditioned day in, day out since the age of 9 that I had no strength to get away. I was regularly threatened into believing that if this secret came out, I would be the one punished. The brainwashing of the little girl, the fear instilled from a very young age was just as present at 26 as it was at 9.

This strong belief that the abuser had the ultimate power over me which he assured I was reminded of by his omnipresence in my life was enough for me to keep quiet and live on with shame and guilt. It does not surprise me when I hear that survivors have waited decades before speaking about the abuse by priests for example. I always defend them as people who have no idea of what it is like to go through this hell, casually comment: 'Why didn't they say something earlier?'. Unfortunately for Nicolas, I also had the excellent memory of an elephant and could fill pages out at the police station with details, even of the abuse that happened 16 years prior. An elephant never forgets.

I had the stubborn will to live on despite carrying a heavy load within me during years of silence. If you believe that your life is no longer worthwhile and that you cannot continue, let me tell you that you very well can. You too have the inner strength and determination to see it through. Disappearing from this planet only means that your abuser wins. You will cling on to life because you are worthy and deserving of living a joyful and peaceful life and one day you will report the criminal who has attempted to destroy you and get the justice for yourself and for that little child that lives on within you.

Gradually, Nicolas lost more and more control of his possession over me and became genuinely worried that I may speak out. My sister, Denise who lived with me at the time, was used to reporting my every move to our father on a daily basis. She was his little spy. Even in my apartment, Nicolas would casually lock the door of my bedroom to freely abuse me while Denise was revising in the room next door, not in the slightest bothered by what was happening a few metres away from her.

One night, when I was already sleeping, Nicolas asked Denise to steal my car keys and give them to him. She did that without questioning the morals of such behaviour. He took my car and changed the ownership over to Elena, another sister, in Luxembourg. A few weeks before, I had gone back home, and Nicolas hid my car keys. I needed to go back to the UK to work and Nicolas made me sign a blank contract, with which he then fabricated a 'contract' later, stating that I was apparently selling my car to Elena. On that same visit, he also told Elena and Denise to hide my phone. They obeyed without questioning any demand that he asked of them, like they were programmed robots. Nicolas said he would not give me the car keys or my phone back unless I signed that blank contract. Elena could then easily change the ownership of the car.

Unbeknown to any of them, I had a copy of my car key with me in the UK. Nicolas even followed me to the UK to catch me as he had felt that he was slowly losing control over me. He stormed into my workplace and demanded to speak to me. Searching for me in the laboratory, I'm so thankful I wasn't there as things escalated from then on. I had a gut feeling that he had gone after me, so I fled to Luxembourg. Back home, I asked my mother where my two sisters had gone with my car. I then drove to the forest, where my mother told me that both sisters were jogging and took back my car that they had stolen from me. I went to the nearest police station to ask how to change the ownership back to my name as I was still paying a loan on that car. My doing this, unnerved Nicolas for probably the first time, as it felt that the scales of control were changing. The sisters had contacted him to tell him that I had taken the car. He threatened me aggressively on the phone and asked me to do the 'right thing'. The irony of it. I was very unsure as to how much harm he would have inflicted upon me if he had physically caught up with me in his sinister rage.

I was asked questions about the car and the police officer called Denise and Elena to the station. They reluctantly came and sat opposite me. It was very tense and uncomfortable between us. With a straight face, Elena said that I had sold the car to her and that I had received the money as per contract. Many people can lie without an ounce of suspicion. She was very practised and good at it. Finally, the officer told me that he was sorry, but I had to give the key back to Elena as it was 'her' car. That was the tipping point that made my glass overflow. The 'car incident' will always be known as the blatant trigger that brought such infuriating injustice to smack me directly in the face, with the culprits sitting right in front of me, lying through their teeth.

With no warning, without planning it in my head beforehand, I snapped. I had finally been pushed to my limit and saw red as the years of torture ran through as visuals in my mind at great speed. No more could I keep this burden to myself, no longer was I prepared to suffer in silence and bear the immense strain. Bursting into anger I began to verbally unravel in detail to the two sisters, who felt like strangers, sat in front of me, about how their father abused me for 16 years. I mentioned the sordid details that normally would have shocked any person hearing it. The reaction from the sisters after my emotional admission was to smile. The officer was very surprised at their reaction as it was just inhumane. Their only verbal response to the horrid allegations I had just poured out for the first time in 16 years was for Denise to reveal that 'Papa has done so much for you, and you would not professionally be where you are today if it was not for him, you owe him'. Elena confirmed Denise's statement and added that I should be happy that I didn't get pregnant and that I am discrediting all the REAL victims of abuse by lying.

The police officer went out of the room for a few minutes to make copies and left the three of us alone. The two sisters looked at me with a smile, their legs crossed. They casually asked me whether I had bought new shoes. They liked them a lot apparently. Let's put this into context. This is after I had, moments before, burst out with details of the abuse that were not easy to digest. I was crying quite extensively the whole time, a mix of fear, deep sadness, fury and relief all rolled into a mass of emotion, and all they could say was that my new shoes looked pretty, as though we had been enjoying small talk. Their insensitive and callous reaction is the result of them being prepared for years beforehand by Nicolas, that one day, I would come up with something against him. Since I was 'mentally unstable' like our mother, it was to be considered a total lie.

Their reaction portrayed none of the emotions one would expect, such as shock, disgust or empathy. At one point the officer got very irritated by my sisters and told them to stop smiling – did they not realise that their sister was suffering, and their smile was inappropriate? During the encounter, Denise called our father, who wished to speak to the police officer. He asked him exactly what I had said. That man was omnipresent. He was trying very hard to make sure that his 'secret' hadn't come out, but slowly it had. The closed drawer had just burst out all over the place and now the process had been started.

My car was then handed back to Elena, and I stayed behind at the police station. I could not believe that I had just disclosed for the first time what had happened to me since my childhood. It was very surreal, and I felt very disconnected from reality, as in a trance state attempting to make sense of what I had just said out loud. It was as if by verbalising the abuse for the first time in so many years, I was only then realising how grave it was. It felt like for the first time I had become conscious of it, right there at the police station. Prior to this encounter, I had never envisioned that this moment could ever become a reality. The car incident was the last drop, that made the vase spill over. It was that extreme feeling of injustice, the accumulated pain that made me burst in that police station.

'I am not a baker, and I can't simply ignore what I just heard' said the police officer with full empathy towards me. He immediately wrote a name and number on a post-it and referred me to the main investigator in Luxembourg city. He said if I don't contact him, he will have to as it was his duty. I was very lucky to have been in the presence of a police officer who was sensitive enough about the topic of child sexual abuse to not let me walk away from this police station without following up on the case. If it wasn't for him, I would certainly not be alive today after that painful encounter with my sisters. I don't know what my enraged abuser would have been capable of, especially after me revealing his dirty secret for the first time in 16 years. If I had not killed myself, he most likely would have gotten rid of me, one way or the other.

The same day and the following days, I was bombarded with text messages and emails from Nicolas and my siblings. They were telling me that they are now at a point of no return and that I should, for the love of God 'do the right thing'. Nicolas, full of rage, in his messages, accuses me of being a sexual abuser, a chronic drug abuser and that I am a sadistic heartbreaker. I am supposedly seducing men to then watching them suffer. He concludes one of his emails by declaring *I am more than a good father, full of sexual power, even at my age, but I am not an animal.*

One day after the infamous 'car incident', I had to reopen drawers in my mind, that had been tightly shut for 16 years. Horrid details of the abuse were spoken out loud, for the first time ever. They were not only being verbalised in a one-to-one setting, but they were being video recorded, so that they could be watched again and again. It's as if I was being endlessly violated. These tapes are somewhere and have also been viewed by my abuser, whose only reaction was to ridicule me when he referred to the video recordings during his defence in court. The feeling of losing control with regards to who has or will be watching me verbalising disgusting details of the abuse with my tears, flowing down my face is unbearable.

It was surreal. It's as if prior to that, I was living in a detached state, only surviving, day by day, without really being connected to reality. It's as if I had had two realities all my life. The reality, in my head, in which everything was fine and there was no wrong being done to me, each day. I was a good student, the abuse can't have been that bad, then, right? The other reality, however, was the real one unfortunately, in which my survival mechanism was keeping me from feeling. My body and mind were fully disconnected, to not face that cruel reality, in which I was being physically, psychologically, and sexually abused.

Following the encounter at the police station, Nicolas, in another email threatens that he will be distributing 500 copies of a letter depicting his daughter as *what she truly is* in a popular location in Luxembourg city, if I don't behave. He says that he considers me now as mentally deranged and that if I don't conform, he would be informing the medical society of Luxembourg of my condition. He also warns me that he will charge *a lawyer of top quality of course* and that this incident at the police station will cost me my future, that my employer will surely fire me and that I will never find another job here in Luxembourg because of my unruly behaviour.

Even though I was somehow relieved, I was very scared of what Nicolas would do to me. A few days later, he stormed into my workplace in Luxembourg and started looking for me as he did in the UK. My employer at the time protected me and let me hide in the basement during the encounter. The following day, I received a message from my family who kindly arranged for a catholic priest Father Marcus from Paris to visit me in order to exorcise me of all the demons that possessed me. They were apparently responsible for all this 'nonsense' I had told the police. I started receiving death threats from my younger brother Leonard, telling me that he was now at a point of no return. From every side, I was being threatened and told that I should retract what I had said or else I would regret it.

Luxembourg, 1993

The Power of Conditioning

Chapter Seven

The Criminal Investigation

As one can imagine, writing this book is not an easy task for a victim of these atrocities. I will never 'get over the abuse', regardless of the years that pass. I have learnt to divert my mind whenever I get flashbacks from the past and I still have reflexes that may be 'strange' for people, but for me they are rationally justifiable considering the trauma. I have only recently noticed that I always hold both of my hands in tight fists. It wasn't until someone pointed it out to me, that I became aware of it. I never realised that I was always so tense, ready to fight danger.

My body had been conditioned to always be ready, just in case. I could never fully relax and my fists, even when lying in bed, were a residual reaction. I now consciously open up my hands when I feel that I am back in fighting mode. The danger is not imminent anymore and the body needs to catch up with that realisation.

Many people wrongly think that I am cured, that I am 'over' the abuse and can freely talk about it, simply because I took the step to openly and publicly speak out about this silent pandemic that is the reality for far too many children. Since sexual violence is often invisible and you can't see bruises from the outside, the pain is internalised and accentuated by the intense feeling of shame and guilt that accompanies this type of crime.

Many journalists dare to ask me details of the abuse and thereby trespass my boundaries. They misunderstand their limits and navigate towards voyeurism and sensational journalism. Depicting details of the abuse in a newspaper article will have no added value in showing the gravity of the crime, other than triggering me and setting my healing back. I will always be the one controlling my narrative when I speak about what happened to me, not the other way around.

The dirty actions of a criminal decades ago, still impact my everyday life in the form of PTSD since I have lived in constant fear. I hear, see and feel intensely because I have learnt to anticipate danger. I am always steps ahead in my mind in preparation. This adaptive mechanism has allowed me to survive the unimaginable. As far as I can remember, I have been labelled as 'strange' and many other variants of this pejorative term. I could rationally understand why people, even those who considered me as a 'friend', would feel this way about me. They often mocked me, because they found me naive and a little 'dumb', despite my academic successes.

I was often looked down upon, perhaps driven by

people's jealousy. I did not understand people's second-degree jokes. I lived in a parallel world, in my head most of the time to escape the painful reality. I have always felt totally out of place in relation to my peers, I never belonged. It's like I had a different vision of this world we live in; as if I was born with a mind of an old person. I also grew up, feeling that my worth as a human being was less than that of the people surrounding me.

Today, I stand proud with my sticker of 'weird', 'special' and 'strange'. I am glad to not conform to what society expects of me. I am looking at these labels as an asset, rather than a weakness and am therefore able to fully embrace my potential by not following the crowd. From experience, it works, I can fully be me, unapologetically, every day.

Try it. Feel free to just be you! In this sense, I believe that our role as parents is to merely accompany our children through life. If they fall, we catch them. Society has us conditioned, however, that our duty is to shape them in order to quietly fit into society's rigid moulds and if they do not fit the norms, to quickly label them. We put brakes on their creativity by trying hard to make them conform without realising that we are actually preventing them from reaching their full potential. These future adults will more often, than not, end up being miserable, disconnected from their intuition and misaligned with who they are supposed to be in life.

I have embarked on a painful mission by writing this book, to dig up the criminal records from 2009-2013. I have gone down to the basement and retrieved them after ten years of ignoring them. This book, the push for justice for my mother, however, is worth having to face the heavy past again. It's for a good cause and sometimes one needs to suffer to be able to heal as I have repeatedly learnt. Healing will never be possible in this case, but damage control is the best achievable outcome when it comes to child sexual abuse.

The morning of his arrest, two weeks after the event at the police station, Nicolas received a visit from police officers performing a house search. The policemen reported that my mother was indifferent and did not in the slightest wonder what they were doing at her home. No surprise there, as she was relentlessly kept silent with the heavy antipsychotics. She kept watching TV while they were looking for evidence for the crime her husband was accused of. Nicolas was asked where he slept in that house and he answered, *sometimes here, sometimes there.*

Nicolas was called to the police station to defend himself against my allegations. He starts by telling his life story about how he ended up in Luxembourg via Dubai and the UK. He tells the investigator how, despite being a pharmacist, he had also worked in other business sectors. He says that ten years ago now, he switched domains and found a niche in the stamp market. He usually trades online and only earns little money from it. He has apartments in Cyprus and Greece, from which he drives his online sales.

He describes how his wife got sick in 1991, due to the sudden death of her father. According to Nicolas, his wife suffers from hereditary schizophrenia, for which she's repeatedly been admitted for. He says the only way he can keep his wife out of hospital for life is to continually put her under psychiatric medication. He proceeds with a tree diagram, in which he carefully depicts his family's lineages, going back to 1875. Evidently, he specifically highlights the family members affected by this supposedly hereditary schizophrenia, me included.

He then responds to the allegations.

Everything that Mary accuses me of is false...she has always been incontinent and that's why I needed to go to her bed each night...

I have never slept in her bed, so I could never have woken up next to her, logically!

Anyone stating the opposite, must be lying.

I have always supported my eldest daughter because she was special...

She was always bullied by her five siblings and therefore developed an inferiority complex.

Mary is depressed and she always thinks that she is the best...

...she can't stand anyone contradicting her.

I am a father who always needs to know second by second where my children are...it is for their safety, especially Mary.

I need to make sure she doesn't get into trouble, so I must control her every move.

Mary is an extremely shy, open-minded girl who has severe psychological problems.

My wife and children discriminated her...

Yes, I used code words with her to communicate but they were not in any way sexually connoted.

...all I did was medical, and my daughter misunderstood my care.

The day after his arrest, Nicolas was able to have some time to think about what had happened the day before. He was then questioned again, this time by the judge.

I have never done anything wrong, and I have no criminal record.

Mary is like a role model for the other sisters as they have all followed in her footsteps.

She is a very jealous girl and a big liar.

She never thinks before doing, her actions are irrational. For example, she would be capable of jumping from a window if she had a problem, without thinking...

...she knows the Luxembourgish laws very well and she is using them to her advantage. By putting me in prison, she just wants to destroy my business out of revenge.

I never had any issues with her; she always sent me birthday cards.

My family is in perfect harmony, there is mutual respect between the family members.

I have never had any extramarital relations; my wife is the only woman I have ever touched.

Mary has the same condition as my wife; she's the only one who inherited it...

I medically taught my children how to have normal sexual relations...

Over the next days, witnesses were called to the police station. One by one, the siblings tried to repeat the version of the story that Nicolas was trying to convey, in panic, before he was finally arrested. I am so glad to have so many siblings who contradict each other, entangling themselves in the multiple versions of their father's 'truth'. A small glimpse of some of the statements is shown in the following pages.

Andreas gave two police statements, one glorifying his father and the other one bashing him. Of course, his credibility was impacted, and he could not be trusted anymore to be telling the truth. His first statement was taken a few days following his father's arrest.

My sister's accusations against our father are false and I strongly believe that she invented that story to punish him, who was not helping her financially...

I never had a good relationship with my sister as she was always treated like a princess by our father...

I knew the reason why Mary was our father's favourite child; she was wetting her bed at night and so, needed more attention from him...

Our father spoilt my sister, and she received every present that she had ever wished for...

She was the only one allowed to travel abroad with our father...

Mary always acted like the boss in our family during our childhood; she always thought she was the best one...

When our mother got sick, Mary insisted on taking over her role when she was 9 years old... Mary had no interest in our mother, because she was selfish and only thought about herself...

Mary was dirty and stinky and rarely showered...at home, she was always teased by her five siblings and our father would tell us to stop ganging up on her...

...Mary is a born actress; she can laugh and cry on command...

...she is a liar since birth and has psychological issues. I believe she also has an inferiority complex...

...I remember that at home, it was all about Mary, everyone had to eat what Mary wanted, we could not watch TV, because Mary was revising and so, on... besides, she only succeeded in school because she was a liar, and she could learn by heart...

My siblings told me that Mary had financial issues and that this is the only reason, why she was accusing our father of sexually abusing her; I fully believe that too...

...I admit that I was jealous of Mary, but kept that to myself and have never disclosed it until today...I have always had open communication with our father...

...I can't believe Mary could do something like this to our father...

...Our father has done everything for his children and wife; he would give his last shirt to his children if he had to...

...Mary only thinks about herself and it's only thanks to us that she managed to get a degree...

...even if my father had sexually abused my sister, which I can't believe he had, but even if he had done, I would always support my father. For us, family and religion are sacred and in case someone brings dishonour upon his family, like Mary did, then she shall not have a family anymore...

At that point, Andreas was dating a girl who, somehow managed to open his eyes, to consider 'what if' his sister was telling the truth, and his father was really a child molester? A few months following his first statement, Andreas decided to revisit the principal investigator to retract his first statement in favour of his father and submit a new one to overwrite the previous one.

...I would like to rectify my first testimony as I've had time to reflect about everything and my girlfriend thankfully opened my eyes...

...I now also have contact with Mary and understand many things better than I did before...

...my father is a special person. He doesn't tolerate anyone contradicting him and wants everyone to do as he orders...

I admit that I have always had trouble with my father, and I have never agreed with his life philosophy...

...my father has never hit me but has always threatened to kick me out of the house.

I can only imagine that Andreas' mind at that point was still in denial of the violence he was subjected to as a child and teen as he was not only hit, but he was also repeatedly burnt on bare skin with cutlery held in an open flame!

My father always humiliated me in front of my siblings as the ultimate loser and that they should take a lesson to not follow suit.

I have always had a bad relationship with Mary...

Following conversations, I had with her after our father was arrested, I now realise that he contributed to the hatred my siblings felt towards Mary, growing up.

...my father's parenting methods were very dubious, and it was his way, or no way! His word was always the law...

My father always talked about sex, but in a 'medical' way. He made sure we were fully scared of either falling pregnant or impregnating a girl.

I remember how, despite me being in the same class as Mary during secondary school, my father forbade me to have contact with her; he explained that Mary could revise better if I didn't talk to her...

After I spoke to Mary, I tried to convince the other four siblings to hear me out and not blindly follow our father and just obey without questioning him...

...instead, I was also attacked by them for siding with Mary...I got threats from the siblings which I am submitting to the police...

...I wouldn't be surprised if my siblings, had been lying for their father or took their father's truth at face value...

Today, I understand things better and truly believe that my father tried to isolate Mary, to prevent her from speaking about what he was doing to her...

That statement was given by Andreas fourteen years ago. Since then, he has, despite a criminal conviction, shown public adoration for him. He remains in the shackles of this never-ending pursuit of being 'good enough' in his father's eyes. He is forever impacted by the 'loser' label that his father stuck on his forehead. He will not hesitate to do anything to get his father's clap on his shoulder.

...Mary fully invented the allegations, and our father has never done what he's being accused of.

It's true that our father created a blank contract which he forced Mary to sign, or he wouldn't return the car...

I don't believe my father was doing something wrong when he did that. It was Mary's punishment for not coming home often enough while doing her PhD in the UK. For me, this was logical and normal...

My father told me and my siblings that Mary is a serial liar...

Denise, recalling the incident at the police station...

...Mary started talking about sexual abuse and asked me and Elena what we would have have done if our father had sexually abused us?

...I know Mary very well and knew that she would come up one day with a sexual abuse story as that crime was hard to prove...

...Mary wasn't really upset or distressed; it was all show...

...when we were young, our father always protected Mary because we were not always nice to her...

...Mary has psychological issues; she has a special relationship with our father...

...my father has made such a big sacrifice for his children, and we must respect our parents and follow their orders...

...because of our mother's sickness, my father had to play both roles: mother and father.

...I have always found Mary 'strange' and I can't understand her reactions.

...I don't think it was wrong of my father to write all these letters from prison to ruin my sister's reputation, Mary deserved it...

...it's so unfair that Mary accuses our father, during a time where I am meant to prepare for my exams...

...my father is very generous and sacrificed everything for his children...

...my father would never threaten my sister and if he did then he's a hypocrite...

...it is scientifically proven that a man of 55 years of age can't have an erection...

...if my father sexually abused my sister then he is not normal in my eyes and must be punished...

...Mary was my absolute best and only friend, but she could not tolerate that her little sister could possibly be as smart as her...

...I never wanted Mary's car and I found my father's reaction towards Mary quite extreme...

...Mary was very distressed at the police station; she was crying and talking at the same time...I had never seen her that upset before...

...I told her that she should be happy that she didn't get pregnant as she's discrediting all the real rape victims.

...I was just kidding when I said that because I couldn't believe a word, she was saying...

...Mary is a drug addict and since she's a pharmacist, she has access and knowledge...

...Mary was the only one who had problems and so needed more attention from our father.

My mother was then also questioned and had obviously been briefed by her five children to stick to one storyline. She had forgotten the original version and answered the questions with full honesty. She contradicted her children's testimonies.

She describes how I was her husband's favourite daughter and that he bought me everything that I asked for. She says that I was lovely and kind. She confesses that she never really wanted six children, that she and her husband always used contraception and yet, she always ended up pregnant. She then talks about her regular unconsented psychiatric hospital admissions for which, she didn't know the reason of. She mentions that she takes many sleeping pills.

Two months following his arrest, Nicolas got up one morning and had a great idea. From his prison cell, he wrote a letter, again, using only capital letters to my PhD mentor in the UK. He wanted to 'update' my supervisor about my 'crimes'. He obviously omitted to mention that the address on the envelope was that of the largest prison in Luxembourg. It must have been an honest mistake, right? Nicolas states that I stole my sister's car and that he involved the police. He says that the dean of the university, where I was doing my PhD at, has been notified about my wrongdoings.

He warns that he also informed the police in the UK about his daughter being a thief. He says that he has launched a disciplinary action at the pharmaceutical society in Luxembourg and the UK against me for grave professional misconduct, drug abuse, theft, and unethical treatment of animals in the laboratory. He then describes me in detail as to why I am not fit to practise my profession. He adds that my supervisor should be careful when dealing with me as I am truly a big liar. He concludes his letter by asking my supervisor whether he can give him my address in the UK and that he's very sorry to confirm this sad news, *but Mary can only blame herself for the mess she put herself in.* Later during the trial, Nicolas made up a whole story about me having a love affair with that same PhD supervisor.

Questioned about the continuous letters, that he sent everywhere to ruin my reputation, Nicolas answered that he was only doing his duty as a father. He needed to inform the authorities about his daughter, who has a toxic lifestyle, putting her patients at risk. He says that he had sent many warnings to me before finally deciding to make an official complaint. His main aim was apparently to protect me from myself.

Nicolas is asked about the statement that Andreas

made in favour of his sister and against his father. His only reply was that Andreas is lying and that indeed, I was discriminated by my own family and hated by my mother. He says that I needed more attention than the others because of my 'condition'. According to him, I was not his favourite but he saw me as his patient, that he needed to protect.

He then says that his wife, also has the same psychiatric condition as his daughter, which started in 1991 and according to him, this is the only reason why he finds himself in prison right now.

The judge then questions the contradicting stories of his five children. Nicolas admits that he just can't remember telling what information to what child, that his memory is failing him. Nicolas is adamant that he is innocent and that his daughter invented these allegations, only to harm him. He says that my only aim is to gain money from it, nothing else. He is also sticking to his version of the story, that I voluntarily sold my car to Elena and that I knew what the consequences were. He then describes me as egocentric, pretentious, and entitled.

In another statement, Nicolas insists that he is a good person, that he is respected all around the world. He repeats that he did nothing wrong, and the others are always causing him trouble but he's Christian enough to forgive everyone. He is asked why his other five children have been threatening Mary while he's in prison. He answers that it is normal that his children see him incarcerated and that they show resistance to the one who caused this trouble.

He pledges that his daughter has plainly made up this story and that anyone could do that. He just needs access to the internet, and he would ultimately prove his innocence. He adds that Mary obviously falsified all the emails. He gets angry during the interrogation with the judge and tells her that she is violating his human rights as well as refusing a confrontation between him and his daughter to clarify the 'misunderstanding'.

He tells the judge that she has no idea how much he loves his daughter and that is why he needs to have a meeting with her. The judge then presents him with another letter that he sent from his prison cell to my employer. He says that he promises not to do that anymore and that he *will try to remove Mary from his mind.*

He says that I am particularly interested in these types of sexual allegations and that I am an actress and love imitating people. According to him, I was very fond of the love affair between Bill Clinton and Monica Lewinsky and so, this would explain where I got my inspiration from. *Since Mary started the prosecution, she is now too ashamed to admit she lied; she is scared to go to prison.*

Nicolas then goes on about how I love taking advantage of my 'sexual dominance' towards men. He then gives an example to demonstrate his hypothesis. He says that he found an invoice which 'proves' that I slept on my own in a hotel room adjacent to my PhD mentor's room when we came to Luxembourg for a scientific conference. Nicolas believes that the only reason I came up with the allegations was to harm the family and remove him as the key family member.

He says that he needs to be released from prison and that would make Mary very happy and relieved. Besides, the other family members would welcome her back in the family if the judge was to let him go. A few months following his arrest, Nicolas describes his life story to the judge. He says that he loves writing and that he wants her to have a broader idea about the whole story of his family.

...in 1985, I was a chief pharmacist in Dubai, my wife was an established doctor and we decided to get a Benelux visa. I did not know where Luxembourg was... My wife told me Belgium I know, the Netherlands I know, so we had better visit Luxembourg. I agreed, I never refuse any request from my wife...arriving in Remich, my wife left me at the hotel with Andreas and Mary (4 and 2 years old) and she came back after 3-5 hours. She said to me, she will never leave Remich and if I really love her, then I should leave her with Andreas and Mary in Remich and I should return to Dubai alone. I thought she was joking, but it was a real final decision from her side.

...I returned to our flat in Surrey, UK and one week

later I tried to arrange the move to Luxembourg. Back in Dubai, I started to work again, and my wife got pregnant with Denise, who was born in the UK. My wife called me daily, asking me to move to Remich, she was dreaming of that place. I have done my best to make her forget about her wish, but I really failed. I never say no to my wife, we have real mutual love, she never puts pressure on me and neither do I; I never put pressure on her...5 complete years, we fed each other like lovers, food and drink, even coffee and tea, even at the restaurant or when we were visiting friends. No one could understand our love feelings. She is the first woman I touched in my life and the last woman I will ever touch in my life...

We married accidentally, she was supposed to marry another man, and I was only invited to the wedding ceremony, but I became her husband, not him. My wife was uncertain of my love for her. I never pressured her for sexual intercourse. I learnt to respect females, to value them as humans and not as a body to use.

I got a real feeling and understanding for the most sacrificing partner in a male-female relationship, being the woman. So, I travelled to the UK and joined my wife and three children in Luxembourg. My wife refused to leave Remich and we have lived in Luxembourg ever since.

After going into great details as to why his daughter Mary urgently needs a psychiatric evaluation, he concludes his letter with these words:

...please help Mary recover physically first then you will get a whole new Mary without any psychiatric disorder. I would love to see Mary joking and happy. A good healthy brain is only possible in a good healthy body.

Myself, 3 months in prison in a real healthy way of living, regularly eating three times a day, promenade one hour a day, full body control, flat foot pads, sleeping at a regular time. I got a real new feeling, even my wife confirmed my health improvement, even my psychic condition improved. Even if it is a prison, still I get the spirit of joke and happiness, the only problem is to be locked up for 18 hours. I feel I am a new, fresh Nicolas, not the one arrested in July...

Nicolas then adds a page, in which he reiterates his unique name, in capital letters of course.

NICOLAS IS MY NAME

UNIQUE NAME WORLDWIDE

ONLY ME GOT THAT NAME, THAT NAME IS ME

SO ONLY ONE NELLY WORLDWIDE MARRIED TO NICOLAS

ONLY ONE ANDREAS GOT FATHER NAME NICOLAS

ONLY ONE MARY GOT FATHER NAME NICOLAS

ONLY ONE DENISE GOT FATHER NAME NICOLAS

ONLY ONE LEONARD GOT FATHER NAME NICOLAS

ONLY ONE ELENA GOT FATHER NAME NICOLAS

ONLY ONE MIRA GOT FATHER NAME NICOLAS

ONLY ONE VERONIQUE IS NICOLAS' LAWYER

ONLY ONE HER EXCELLENCY MADAME DOROTHY IS NICOLAS JUDGE

PLEASE SEARCH 'NICOLAS' ON GOOGLE, SO YOU CAN WATCH MY WEDDING CEREMONY WITH NELLY, I WAS 29 YEARS OLD AND SHE WAS 24.

THANKS TO NELLY'S CHOICE OF LUXEMBOURG TO LIVE AND RAISE SIX KIDS

NELLY WAS RIGHT, 100 % FOR HER CHOICE, REAL PROTECTION AND SECURITY, NOT ONLY FOR OUR SIX KIDS BUT ALSO FOR NELLY & ME

SO, THANKS TO LUXEMBOURG!!!

In another entertaining letter to the judge, Nicolas pleads for his release. He explains how he *was transported with great respect in a lovely van, very comfortable, with two kind policemen.* He says that he was examined at the hospital with the most sophisticated endoscope and that he enjoyed seeing his intestines on the screen. He continues: *Yes, I am a pharmacist, but never visited any doctor in Luxembourg for 23 years, except a dentist, not even when I had a FATAL car accident. My brain was shaken, black vision with golden stars and I lost 100 % consciousness, but I* could hear my kids crying 'daddy died' and 30 minutes later, I was totally fresh again, no one of us got injured.

...Still, I remember you handing me my letter to the medical society, and I hear your voice: Mr E., you are damaging your daughter's future. So, I am not only feeling shy, but also ashamed. YOU CHANGED ME. So, I decided to behave in a real Luxembourgish way forever with full respect to everybody. To be Luxembourgish is not easy but the road of 1000 km, starts with the first metre, even the first centimeter, even the first millimeter. It is a decision. The lost boy in the Bible said NOW, I go to my father and me, after seeing you on 2nd of October, I said now, I will start my way towards my respectful Luxembourgish way. So, thank you, thank you, THANK YOU. I would love to do a PhD like Mary did, I already asked the University of Luxembourg to enrol me.

...I would like to extend the level of expertise of my daughter Mary:

- Determination of drug abuse, I can prove that her drug abuse caused her physiological and pathological disorders, which leads to her long history of real psychiatric disease

- Confirmation that Mary has full freedom since the age of 12, she went with her class to Austria for 10 days. When she was 12-15 years old, she always played football in the streets, only with boys, out at 4pm, back at 9pm.

- Then Mary locked herself up from 15-18 years old, always studying, she loved to be good at school. So, as a father, I gave her lovely support, so she always received certificates of excellency.

- Age 18-19, first year, totally living alone, EVERY weekend, she got at least TWO boys staying overnight, Saturday until Monday morning. Example: 24-year-old Iranian boy and 22-year-old Japanese boy, always with Mary, daily, almost living with her.

...I apologise for my hunger strike; I know it is childish. I am a 60-year-old father of four children, who still need my support, my wife almost invalid, needs my company. Surely, Mary's allegations will be respected, and trial will determine reality!

...I promise you 100 %, no more contact to Mary before or after trial or maybe if one day, she changes her way and wakes up to reality, so I will accept if she contacts me first. I am finally in reality now, Mary is now out of my mind, I wish her all the best success and a bright future.

...even if you leave me in Prison all my life, I will always love Luxembourg.
On the same page, Nicolas continues:

Many times, I try to disconnect myself from Mary to let her be independent, but she always wants to be friends again. My reply was 'Mary, you have to stop acting like a liar'. If you ask her friends, they all describe Mary in *one word: LIAR, a real clever LIAR. She manipulates everyone and everything. She is perfect at that. She hacks my account and changes my passwords. A pharmacist like her cannot be a liar, it is too dangerous. Put Mary in front of you and you will know who Mary really is.*

Mary is my biggest building block in all my six kids, I never tolerate any harm to her. I prefer even NO LAWYER at all during the trial, to be sure nothing will hurt Mary. Maybe I will ask my current lawyer to resign, because it seems she does not understand my English writing. I LOVE LUXEMBOURG MORE THAN ANYONE IN THIS WORLD, IN PRISON OR OUT. Nicolas

...I forgive Mary and everybody, I say what Jesus said on the cross: Please God, forgive them, because they don't know what they are doing.

...In my point of view, I am the single richest individual in Luxembourg stamps, in volume and rarity. My only hope is to establish an electronic stamps museum for Luxembourgish stamps and postal history. I got what nobody worldwide has – Luxembourgish postal history. So do not worry that I will escape Luxembourg. I am a big lover of Luxembourg. I hope you can believe me.

The following is a small excerpt from the complaint letter written by my abuser from his prison cell and personally signed and deposited by both my sisters Denise and Elena at the medical society in Luxembourg. As instructed by their jailed father, without any ethical consideration, their only intention was to ruin my professional reputation and ultimately, get me struck off the medical register. A similar letter was also sent to the pharmaceutical society in London, with the same aim, to get me to lose my professional licence.

Dear Sir Madame.

- Mary is apdekteh. in schutrange.
- Mary go to Disc up to 4-5 am. and immediately she start Duty in the Morning with No Relax
- I see Mary Not in proper form to behave as lux-pharmacist can cause risk on patient.
- Mary Not at stable psychic — I.E.

- Being declared to police petange she attempt suicide on 7/11/09 on Her Birthday over dispute with Her Father [me]

- May be further meeting with Mary as College Medical to determine capability of Mary to practice safely Her J.B Specialy Schutrange pharmacy prefer Mary for pharmacy de garde
  → So Mary alone I see not safe for patients especially when she is half sleeping.

So she is so exhausted at UK she working so heavy beside Her study as phD. So risky to practice

DATA   EMAL ADRESS to confirm precise

Writing to the judge, Nicolas apologises for his complaint letter:

...All my life, I will remember that I was such a bad father, who can be a reason for damaging his daughter's professional future. So, in my heart, I have great regret and instant decision to withdraw all the complaints against Mary. I decided to let Mary have her own way of life, not only Mary, but all my other 5 kids, no more interference from me. But always, I give support to all of them, if they ask me.

...I love Mary even more than before because she was a reason for me changing my way, really it is a turning point in my life. Once more, thank you from all my heart and my promise to you and to JESUS, to continue loving Mary exactly as I love the other kids. Even more now than before because she got hurt because of my bad way of communication. It was so bad; Jesus will give me the chance to show Mary my real love. If she visits me here in prison, she will feel that I am really a new Papa.

...If it is allowed, can you give my message to Mary:

My darling Mary,
You are my love and stay my love forever. Please my love, feel nice, safe, quiet, and happy. Please never feel guilty that I am in prison. I respect the way this happened, it shows MATURITY, so maturity leads to lovely responsible person in society. I am a changed man; I withdrew every complaint against you in Luxembourg and the UK.

I know how you are sensitive and how my opinion of you matters to you. I can tell you, it is just LOVE, no less. It will be the greatest gift from Jesus if you visit me in prison, but please if you don't bring SNICKERS, I will be sad. If not allowed to visit me, so just leave a pack of 10 Snickers at the entrance of the prison, marked Nicolas E. Room 143. By the way, I have a very relaxing, luxurious life here.

Today, lunch was a large duck leg, croquettes, Chinese sauce, flan, and ice-cream. Yesterday, was half a chicken, vegetables, large Pink Lady apples. I eat in a lovely room facing the garden. There is daily walking, Church every Sunday, hot shower daily, clothes washed and ironed, bed sheets changed weekly, Signal toothpaste, Sunsilk shampoo, all free, plus 45 euros per month as a gift from our Grand Duke, so shopping is delivered every Wednesday to the room. The mail is collected and delivered to my room. Only real problem is I have no job to do. So, I just watch TV, listen to the radio, and write. My eyes become stronger, no computers, no phones, no internet. My hair starts growing, I am not joking, it is real. I think from the way of life, just relaxing, no stress at all as before. No invoices, no business etc.

My darling, I hope by now, you got your smile back and I am responsible for myself when I declare to you and Jesus, that I got ZERO negative feeling towards you, so it is real declaration.

I feel guilty about the way of communication...so I ask Jesus to give me the chance to show my real love to you.

My darling, don't count on anybody's feeling towards you. You know me very well, how much I love you and always will.
Papa

N.B. Today, I was shopping, and I bought porridge, so I mixed it with milk and some sugar. So I remembered one or two years ago, when you bought porridge from Cora to mix with milk, now you laugh I know. If you loved it, why not?

Be happy my darling Mary

In another letter to the judge, Nicolas explains that because they are a Christian family, the girls MUST be virgins otherwise they can't ever get married. He says this is a fixed reality, it is not culture but Christian superior law. He then continues to explain that he should not be misunderstood, that he is not in favour of this law and that of course, many girls do lose their hymen due to sport and unfortunately, they cannot get married. He then states that both, he and his wife are not allowed to divorce by law, no matter the reason, once married, always married for ever; this is Christian highest law. He gives an exception 'EXCEPT if the husband confirms that his bride was not a virgin, so he can divorce, and she will never get married again, her only solution would be to change religion'

This may sound strange, he writes *but it is a fixed reality, for millions of people*. He continues to explain that because there were eight people in the house, it was too crowded for him to have ever had the opportunity to abuse me. He starts describing each house, we have ever lived in, how many rooms they had and how it was impossible for him to have sexually abused me while living there.

He then writes a whole essay about my virginity and how I supposedly intensively protected it from men. He finishes his letter by reiterating his innocence and that I am a complete liar. He says that his confessions are the only reality, referring to me misunderstanding his 'medical' procedures and in fact, he only saw me as his patient.

Chapter Eight

His Criminal Trial

Since being vocal about sexual abuse in public, I do my best to focus my messages on empowering victims, rather than focusing on the abuse and the abuser *per se*. On the one hand, to avoid triggering myself, I can't be floating in this constant depressing mood, that these flashbacks cause. I need to move forward not backward. On the other hand, I don't want to feed the voyeuristic audience.

Most of the time, the court room is filled with journalists and bored people, looking for some excitement in their lives, but also abusers, who find it stimulating to hear these details. This last category also attends my conferences. They have a 'catch me if you can' attitude, adding to their thrill. Since over 90 % of the abuse happens by someone in the child's circle of trust, these people rarely resemble the image that society has of child molesters. They rarely look shady. They are kind-looking, approachable, charismatic and could even be wearing a tie and suit. Huge work is needed to change society's misperception of what a child molester looks like.

Not only was the trial re-traumatising for me to have to dig up the agonising details of my past, but the public humiliation had a huge impact on me. I gave birth to two of my five children while going through the criminal trial. I was being attacked, shamed, and discredited repeatedly, by my own family. My two babies gave me the strength to get through this calamity. Being pregnant, I never felt alone in front of the judges. The day after each court hearing, the case appeared in the local newspapers. The recurring fear of being humiliated again, despite the intimidating court hearing of the previous day being over and done with, was overwhelming. Of course, the journalists were simply doing their job, but the collateral pain they inflicted on the victim was unnecessary; their articles merely feeding their voyeuristic readers.

Schwere Vorwürfe nach Jahren des Schweigens
Berufungsverfahren: Familienvater wegen sexuellen Missbrauchs einer seiner Töchter angeklagt

Vor dem Berufungsgericht: Mutmaßlicher Inzest
Verteidiger fordert Freispruch

Familienvater muss in Haft
Urteil im Berufungsverfahren um Inzest

Berufungsverfahren um Inzest und sexuellen Missbrauch
„Mutter durch Tochter ersetzt"
Generalstaatsanwaltschaft fordert 15 Jahre Haft ohne Bewährung für beschuldigten Familienvater

> **Anklage fordert Höchststrafe**
> Familienvater war bereits in erster Instanz zu 15 Jahren Haft ohne Bewährung verurteilt worden

> Geschwister im Prozess des mutmaßlichen Inzests gehört
> **„Hatt wollt onsall erofmaachen"**

> Mutmaßlicher Inzestprozess in Berufung
> **Staatsanwaltschaft bleibt bei Antrag: 15 Jahre Haft**

> Strafantrag in mutmaßlichem Inzest-Prozess
> **15 Jahre Haft sollen bestätigt werden**

A tiny glimpse of the public humiliation I was subjected to during the criminal trial.

At each trial, Nicolas would be accompanied by all or some of his five children to support him, translate for him or carry his heavy bags in which he detained THE ultimate proof that I was lying. They would be sitting on the opposite side of the courtroom, full of confidence, avoiding eye contact with me. I was emotionally very distraught at each hearing, and it was as if the abuse was starting all over again.

The sleazy scarf-wearing defence lawyer M.K. would disgrace me, paint me as a downright dirty liar and money-seeking actress. He would do his best to intimidate and break me, shamelessly attacking the heavily pregnant woman sitting in front of him. I am eternally grateful for my lawyer S.V. at the time. She was professional and human. It was an extremely difficult case, but it was worth all the pain to see my aggressor finally handcuffed and escorted to that shielded police van. Honestly, the best day of my life!

Despite the immense guilt that I have felt following my mother's death of not having been able to save her, I do feel a little comfort in knowing that I managed to get rid of our common offender for some time. She was able to live a few years without being admitted to a psychiatric hospital as her criminal was himself admitted to a closed facility, namely the main prison in Luxembourg. I was able to give him a dose of his own medicine by restraining his freedom, just like he did all these years with my mother. Is it karma? Yes. No bad deed will go unpunished. One will always pay for hurting others, always.

I have the satisfaction that Nicolas received the brutal police treatment that my mother was subjected to. Of course, for him it was rightful while for my mother it was very unfair. This should not have happened even once. Despite him being out of the way and locked up in prison, Nicolas still managed to have full control of the five siblings who had access to my mother. They were instructed to keep her under the heavy medication, she had always been on. They made sure that she remained in a living dead state. The siblings, especially Denise and Elena obeyed as usual without questioning their leader. They even made our mother sign a power of attorney, in which she revoked every right to decide with regards to her finances, civil, legal, and medical matters. They could sign any document on her behalf, closely orchestrated by the guru from a distance.

Prison or not, he never lost the respect of his five children, it's like these four years of investigations and trials never happened in their mind. If they had an impact, it would have only reinforced the loyalty and love they felt for their poor father, now to be regarded as a victim and in need of help. They somehow found their purpose in life, to save him.

Looking through the huge folder, I also found hundreds of pages of letters sent by Nicolas from prison. The addressees were as diverse as can be. Apart from the vile letters depicting me as a criminal, the other recipients included his family all over the world, the Grand-Duke of Luxembourg and President Barack Obama.

Writing to the judge, Nicolas writes a whole exposé on sexual penetration. As usual, in capital letters, he explains that he doesn't put spying devices on his children's bodies, nor does he hide cameras in their bedrooms. He says that he is not responsible for his children's sex lives and that he can't be getting the blame if boyfriends can't sexually penetrate his daughters. He has six children and that it is simply impossible for him to control them or when and with whom they have sexual penetration. He firmly states that his six children are totally free in mind and soul, that they fully love him and that they are all sad for him being in prison.

The last sentence reads *Even my love Mary is sad for me.* His children always make their own decisions. Nicolas goes on and says that I am confusing perpetrators; that apparently my past boyfriends sexually abused me, and I am confusing the abusers with him.

He says that he tolerated prison as well as the damage to his business, but he never revealed the real reason as to why he thinks Mary has a problem. He was now ready to disclose the truth. He then goes on about how I should apologise to my boyfriends for hurting them. He promises to never ask for indemnities from the government for his wrongful jailing. He has THE proof to support his latest defence.

Drawing a cross, at the end of his letter: *I am innocent of any abuse or rape to anyone, even a small insect. I am a real Christian; I love to respect and care for people as far as Jesus gives me capacity and privilege to do that. 133 days of prison so far, every single person, guards and prisoners know my way as real lover of Jesus.*

Jesus' way seems to be misunderstood by people sometimes. But who loves Jesus, is enjoying walking the way. I am writing to you, so that you have an idea about Christianity. I was a teacher in Sunday school at church, until the age of 26. We taught Jesus' way of love, sacrifice and forgiveness based on people unknowingly doing bad things. Of course, if they also make a mistake, but involuntarily, so it's nice to forgive. In Dubai, I was the first man to start a Church, which today, has at least 4000 members. I am now five months in prison, and I am sure the guards and prisoners think that I am crazy. But now, I am very sure they know that they know that I am just living Jesus' way. All the prisoners are male, old, and young but I am the oldest here. So, I feel love for all of them, like I feel love for my children, I do not make a difference.

If I have 2 tangerines, I will give them to another prisoner, who loves tangerines. I am also a prisoner, but as far as I can, I apply Jesus' words and put others' needs before mine. I love to clean the prison yard daily. The prisoners throw food from the windows or cigarette remains. One day, an educated prisoner told me:' Do you think by cleaning the yard voluntarily, they will let you out?' So, I replied to him: 'Every time, I kneel to pick up cigarette remains, about 60/day, it is like sport for a 60-year-old man. Besides when I clean the yard, the prisoners will feel happier and respect their prison.

My way is only Jesus' way. Concerning Mary: the only one who can determine my love and respect to Mary, is Mary herself. I do not want that my defence causes any pain to my daughter. Please say to Mary: merry Christmas and a happy new year from papa. His letters are evidently full of crosses to accentuate how Christian he is.

In another letter to *Her Excellency,* the judge, Nicolas sadly announces that he is 'seriously sick' and needs surgical intervention. He says that he is on food, water, medicine strike since the previous day and that he doesn't like doing that because he creates extra work for the prison staff, but he feels he has no choice.

He warns that he has informed Amnesty international and that his next step will be the European Court of Human Rights, as well as a BBC investigation. He specifies that BBC doesn't adhere to data protection and so he warns the judge *that ALL the names in this criminal case will be published, with nationalities and addresses. Mary pushed this case to become very complicated, when in fact there has never been any abuse or rape BUT since a Luxembourgish female pharmacist has deviated from the code of deontology, she will be in trouble following my complaint at the medical society.*

He says that I will be prosecuted for hacking, theft and lying. *Mary is free to accuse me, but she will need proof or logical witness.* He writes that the judge should be happy that he cancelled his complaints against me even though they were all 100 % true, he adds in brackets.

He continues writing that he is a very kind man, a man of promise, a real Christian but that he is NOT NAÏVE. *I promise not to contact Mary or any of her friends, I will just take care of my wife and four children. I will keep this whole affair only between me and my lawyer. I am not the owner of myself, I am owned by my wife, Mira, Elena, and Denise. They need me so I must preserve their future. Mary has a Masters, a PhD and a husband. Andreas has a Masters and a girlfriend. The other four children only have a secondary school diploma and their Papa.* He writes that he is fine with strict controls when he is out of prison, he also wouldn't mind an 'electronic chip'. He says that the police can go through his mails at home, no problem.

He adds *I love Mary, never ever think a moment against her. She knows that and ALL my family say that Mary feels sad that her father is still in prison.* He says that he is happy with any conditional release from prison. *I love prison, yes, but I love my family and my business too...*

A few weeks on, another letter, stating that *Mary is a liar, and it is my duty as a parent to alert the authorities to protect others and Mary herself. If she was really abused, why didn't she tell the police earlier? Abuse and rape only happen to MENTALLY RETARDED men and women, not only women. Mary is only angry with me because I damaged her relationship with Luke, but now she is happy with Felix. She was even happier with Luke, but when Luke didn't want to advance in the relationship, she broke up with him. If you give me internet access, I will provide you with all the proof of what Mary said to Luke. I feel guilt and regret for her age passing without feeling real happiness. I feel guilt and regret for all the pain I caused to Luke.*

So why all that? Because Mary would like to marry officially in church and to be a virgin. It is not her own will. Mary is sick, she needs a full body medical screening. Her blood analysis is very bad. I want a confrontation with my daughter. My wife and I have never talked about sex with our children. We talk in general to all the children and each child catches what they need from the information.

Mary manipulated all the emails; it is so unfair. Give me internet and I will give you proof. Mary is perfect at memorising stories, I have never had interest in Mary's friends, I respect them all, even the au-pairs. Everyone is witness that I wasn't even interested in their faces. You have been misled and it is so unfair.

Mary is a thief; she stole a car from Elena, and you keep me in prison? You can ask her again; Mary is simply misleading you. She is an addict and abuses drugs. She puts pressure on her brothers and sisters and even her mother, they are all witness. Mary is fooling justice, and this is real injustice, opposing my freedom because of your fear of justice obstruction.

When Nicolas was in custody, Andreas got his father into the local news. Why hasn't Nicolas ever kept his promise with his recurrent hunger strikes? He always resumes eating and drinking. Andreas also started a public petition to question the ethics of keeping people accused of crimes in dubious conditions for a long time without trial. That petition never got any resonance from the public. There seems to be a consensus, thankfully. Keeping a man who's at risk of fleeing, locked up during the investigations of a serious crime is fair. Thank you, Luxembourg.

> **À Schrassig sans procès, il a fait la grève de la faim**

Andreas' attempt to get media attention for his father.

At no point did Nicolas ever take responsibility for his crimes. The narcissistic pervert will always jump into the 'victim' position once things get tricky. It's like they are fully disconnected from reality and believe in their deepest core that they have done nothing wrong.

During the investigations and prior to the long trial, a psychiatric evaluation was done on Nicolas to see whether he was suffering from a medical condition that could relinquish him from taking responsibility for his actions. Sadly, for him, this was not the case. This man, in all consciousness was aware of what he was making his victims endure. He could not get a discount for being unable to understand the consequences of his wrongdoings. The report was done a few months following Nicolas' arrest. With an unstoppable urge to speak, he approached the psychiatrist with a friendly handshake.

Nicolas couldn't wait to let it all out and spoke at full speed mixing French and English. While dramatically gesticulating, he rolled his eyes. The expert could not make him stick to a single language; Nicolas was just too eager to tell him everything! He burst into an incoherent monologue without breathing pauses. He was very enthusiastic to finally be given the opportunity to be heard.

He seemed spatially aware and in full understanding of the reason for the consultation. He started talking about his wife, her mental disease, his six children, four daughters, two sons. He informed the doctor that his wife is mentally sick and that her grandfather Andreas was also schizophrenic. Then he added that Andreas' parents were also schizophrenic and that an aunt had died in a psychiatric hospital in Italy. Nicolas concluded the family tree by stating that his daughter Mary was PROBABLY also schizophrenic considering the family history. He proceeded by frantically drawing schematic evidence for the crazy gene, that seemingly only I inherited. *My other children are all perfectly healthy.*

Nicolas told the psychiatrist that he's neither a paedophile nor a homophile. He said he's fully committed to his wife, with whom he has six children and is not interested in other women. He explained, again by means of a drawing that animals in Europe are not free to have sex as they wish. Cows are artificially inseminated and never mate naturally, which Nicolas thought was very unfair. He doesn't know the reason why he is on the psychiatry ward. He was questioned about suicidal thoughts, which made him tear up. He paused. This did not last long as he hysterically continued his bottomless monologue.

The same doctor met Nicolas again after his strike. He states that he is in very good health, never had an accident or surgery. Asked about his drinking habits, he answers that he rarely drinks alcohol and doesn't smoke. He is a good Christian, a teacher, a reader and a mediator. Apparently, he never takes any medication but can produce his own. Despite his three-day hunger strike, he says he feels 'tip top'.

The psychiatrist wants to know more about Nicolas' history. He answers that there was nothing special to mention. Everything was just fine. His parents had everything in place for a carefree upbringing of eleven children. His wife fell in love with Luxembourg on a trip abroad when they lived in the UK. Nicolas wasn't too enthusiastic about the idea of moving but finally agreed. He then says that he started trading fruit and vegetables, followed by 'financial transactions' in Asia, before finally discovering the lucrative business of philately. He also mentions that he is very rich.

Nicolas nervously got back to the main topic of his strike, for which he wrote a letter of complaint to the Grand Duke. He explains to the psychiatrist that he trades stamps on the internet and flies to Greece every week with 50 kg of stamps. His ultimate dream is to open a stamp museum. Speaking about his wife, he says that she does nothing at all. She sits all day on the sofa and watches TV. He is solely responsible for the household and cooking. His children help because they know that their mother is sick. This was normal though as he also respected his parents when he was young.

He is happy, mentally sharp, and not even hungry. He says he drinks a glass of water in the evening and has lost 7 kg. He randomly repeats the story that his wife got mentally sick following the death of her father in 1991. He proceeds with a long list of the symptomatology of his wife's illness. In his wife's family there are many mentally sick people and they only loved money; they didn't know what love was. He says that my mother's brother sexually abused me. His eldest daughter was like a boy. She played football and she was by far not a girl. He never ever slept in her bed. He wanted to help her because she had a great deal of complexes due to her big breasts. She thought everyone was staring at her chest and so she was very embarrassed, he continues.

Nicolas was very lively during the consultation. He laughs and cries at the same time, speaks very fast and randomly jumps from one topic to the other. He is in no way having a psychotic episode and his flow of ideas are logical and controlled. He says that he has accepted his new life in prison and that he is now on day 10 of the hunger strike. He has made peace with God and the world and has learnt to make the best of his current situation. He says, he even loves his new life and is ready to spend the rest of his life in prison. He dreams frequently and is scared of losing his professional license. He cries.

He is making statistics of the smoked cigarettes in prison. He is not mad at his daughter Mary for what she has done to him. He still loves her despite her unfairly accusing him. He retracted his complaint against her as he didn't want to harm her professional reputation. He wishes her all the best in life, especially now that she is isolated from her own family.

He then adds that all the accusations are totally false and that she misunderstood his medical actions towards her as abuse. He just wanted to help her after all. He says that his daughter needed more attention as she had skinny legs and was considered the ugliest of the four sisters and so, she was bullied by her other siblings. All he did, was protect her from the teasing.

The psychiatrist concludes in his report that Nicolas was very frantic, spoke very fast and decided on the topic of his monologue. He was drawing at his convenience to demonstrate his hypotheses. He understood everything correctly and didn't miss any detail. Despite his wild gesticulation, he didn't lose the thread throughout the conversation. There was no evidence of hallucinations, delusions, or any other psychopathologic symptoms. He didn't show any intellectual deficits and was fully capable of space and time awareness. According to the professional, Nicolas is fully sane and can therefore be criminally prosecuted as he undoubtedly understands cause and effect. He is not in any way mentally sick as to not allow him to take responsibility for his actions. The psychiatrist finally states that the dynamic in this family enables intense dependencies to exist and therefore easily allow manipulative influences from the most dominant parent to pursue.

Following his deranged letters with the sole purpose of ruining my professional reputation, Nicolas sent an 'apology' letter to me, in which he wishes me and my little family a bright future and in his N.B. at the bottom of his letter it reads: *if possible, I need a large box of 10 SNICKERS, I love it, Mary knows that very well. Just leave it at the entrance of CPL (Prison in Luxembourg) P2, Room 143. Thanks, villmools Merci!*

Over the years, I have tried to understand why a human being would subject a child to such horrors. One incident is more than enough to mess up that child for life. How can a father hurt his daughter to this extent? Does he truly believe he has done nothing wrong? Does he truly believe that his actions are 'medical' and that it is all for the best of that child? How does a man walk through life, thinking that his actions will remain unpunished? I have read countless books, watched documentaries and interviews, researched, discussed, debated and yet, I remain as clueless as before to understanding the criminal mind.

As my foreword states, I can only expose the HOW and may never fully understand the WHY, but that is already a baby step in preventing the suffering for other children and empowering adults to speak out, freeing themselves from the shackles of what happened to them as a child and/or teen.

Why do men- and some women – molest children? This question is thoroughly researched by Dr. Anna Salter in *Predators*, who like me, is attempting to dissect these people to get the ultimate rationale as to why some people cross this unimaginable ethical barrier. She has become an internationally recognised expert on sexual predators.

After interviewing a number of men who have raped infants as young as five months of age, men who have repeatedly sexually abused pre-schoolers, men who have targeted children under the age of ten, and men who admit to being sexually attracted to them (some of them obsessively so), she still wonders how some experts in the field can remain in the conviction that the blame of child sexual abuse lies with the child and not the offender.

Interviewing child rapists, she notes how they are very far from the image society associates with criminals capable of hurting children in that manner. Speaking of a man who raped an eight-year-old girl so badly, that she had to be hospitalised, Dr. Salter says that nobody in the world including her, would have been able to successfully pick him out as a child molester. This offender seemingly felt anger and intimidation towards children. Asked about his intimidation tactic, he answers that he stares at his victims to make them nervous, the 'I'm going to get you' look. He says this makes the child look like they're lying if they ever dare to disclose the abuse.

The child rapist pursues in saying that this intimidation tactic also works in case the affair lands in a courtroom. He would just stare at his victim to make her nervous enough to make her lie or make her stumble to make people think she was lying. He sounds very convinced that his simple look has the power to discredit the child's statement.

Dr. Salter writes that in the early part of the century, psychoanalytic writers maintained steadfastly that sexual abuse was the child's fault, and not the adult's; that it occurred because aggressive children 'seduced' innocent men. She cites Dr. Karl Abraham, who in 1907 wrote an article entitled 'The Experiencing of Sexual Traumas as a Form of Sexual Activity' in which he declared that 'in a number of cases, the trauma was desired by the child unconsciously, and we have to recognise it as a form of infantile sexual activity'. His reasoning was that 'in all of them, the trauma could have been prevented. The children could have called for help, run away, or offered resistance instead of yielding to the seduction.' *What is astonishing is that Abraham's views were widely shared within the psychoanalytic community.* Dr. Salter writes that *for more than fifty years, from the first quarter of the 20th Century onward, there was a significant school in psychology, that held the belief that sexual assault victims were responsible for their own victimisation.*

Different 'experts' have come forward to make their observations with regards to child sexual abuse public. The following are examples extracted from the book *Predators.*

Such children derive fundamental satisfaction from the relationship and do not completely deserve the cloak of innocence with which they have been endowed by moralists, social reformers, and legislators. Children are unusually charming and attractive, and we need to consider the child as the actual seducer rather than the one seduced. (Psychiatrist Lauretta Bender, 1937)

The absence of any complaints on the part of the daughters indicates that these girls were not merely helpless victims of their fathers' needs but were gratified by the relationship, if not.... active initiators of it. (Dr. Irving Weiner)

The actual consummation of the incestuous relation... diminishes the subject's chance of psychosis and allows better adjustment to the external world. (Matilde W and A. Rascovsky)

Incest may be a positive experience, or at worst, neutral and dull (West Virginia social work professor, 1979)

Dr. Salter notes that offenders do not bear responsibility in these early works. *They are often described as gentle, fond of children and benevolent. Drs Eugene Revitch and Rosalie Weiss called such offenders harmless individuals and their victims...aggressive and seductive children. These authors complained that a group of children exploited a pedophile through accepting gifts and money.*

Thankfully, the blaming of children for child sexual abuse began to fade in the 1970s and 1980s, although it has never fully died out, and Dr. Salter believes it is currently making a comeback. She cites the legal defence of a priest, who sexually abused a six-year-old boy to have claimed that the boy's parents and the boy himself contributed to the abuse due to their 'negligence'.

Another angle is the blaming of the non-offending spouse. As an example, Dr. Salter cites *Irvin Kaufman et al. who claimed that incest was the child's response to abandonment by the mother. Noel Lustig et al. state the mothers to be the cornerstone of the pathological family system,* thereby removing any responsibility from the actual criminals, in this case the fathers.

In another example, Dr. Salter mentions Yvonne Tormes, who described *a group of incest offenders, some of whom had been extremely violent. They had burnt children with hot irons* (hmm...rings a bell?), *locked a mother in a closet while abusing the child and broken a radio over a mother's head. Tormes wrote that the cause of the abuse was the mother's failure to protect her child,* giving the offender exactly 0% of responsibility in the crime.

Today, the notion of a family entity being responsible for incest is far more current than the idea that children are responsible for seducing grown men. As the author of *Predators* notes, putting the blame of the incest on the family, discounts the offender's culpability. Looking at my personal case, I fully agree that the family as a whole is to blame for enabling the abuse to happen over such a long period of time, however, the ultimate responsibility for the crime remains at 100 % to the perpetrator.

My abuse could have been prevented, even stopped. However, the system is fully dysfunctional, and I am not only talking about the family system. The numerous red flags, the schools, the teachers, the nannies, the neighbours, the doctors, the ELEVEN failed reminders from the judge to child protection services to finally go check what was going on in that house. At some point, one of the numerous live-in nannies we had over the years, told Nicolas that she believes that I am sleep-walking. He, of course laughed it off, knowing very well why I spent my nights walking around the house, desperately looking for a safe place to get some sleep. I have been failed by the system, over and over again. I was so very close to ending my life, it was unbearable. No words will do justice to the hell I was going through. How glad I am not to have gone through with it.

Dr. Salter mentions the Association for the Treatment of Sexual Abusers (ASTA), being the largest professional organisation for the treatment of sex offenders in the world. Although many can be treated, there is no known 'cure'. Current methods include cognitive behavioural treatment, possibly reducing re-offense by 50% in the short term.

The author also touches upon the manipulation process that occurs as part of the grooming prior to sexually abusing a child. *The important differences in maturity levels between abuser and victim is paramount, otherwise the manipulation wouldn't work. The child is at a disadvantage here: He or she has no idea of the offender's intentions, no way to know that the affection expressed isn't genuine, and no recognition of the techniques used to manipulate him or her. Most writers who defend pedophilia – Rind, Bauserman, and Levine, for example – simply pretend this kind of manipulation does not occur and that the children and adolescents are equal partners with adults in sexual activities.*

Over the years of investigations and trials, Nicolas had about five different lawyers, some of them left him, because they could not, in good conscience, defend this offender, who revealed himself as repugnant.

Despite Felix witnessing my deepest vulnerability during the years of investigations and trials, he did not hesitate to hire one of the numerous lawyers who defended Nicolas. Both Felix and Nicolas consulted that same lawyer on multiple occasions with only one aim in mind: to break me. Both Felix and Nicolas sent me the bailiff home a few times to intimidate me and my children. It did not matter to Felix whether the mother of his five children was heavily pregnant, going through chemo and radiotherapy or recovering from a complicated surgery, he did not feel any shame or guilt disrespecting her to that extent.

Chapter Nine

His Present

During his time in prison, which ended up being a cumulative four to five years as opposed to the fifteen years the judges had initially decided on, Nicolas discovered his ultimate artistic vein. One early morning, while doing his rounds in the prison courtyard, he thought to himself, what a great idea it would be to pick up cigarette butts, one by one, from the ground, mindlessly thrown away by fellow inmates after smoking.

As the great justice advocate, he is known for, he just could not bear to see humans destroying Mother Earth and decided there and then to embark on a planet-cleaning adventure. Quite a brilliant thought indeed. Day after day, butt after butt, he did not miss a single one. Sometimes he would stand next to a smoking fellow prisoner and impatiently wait until he finished taking his last puff. He just could not wait to catch the remainder of that burnt cigarette.

He ended up filling a bag full of hundreds of butts, singlehandedly collected on prison ground. One day, without thinking twice, Nicolas aligned the used butts next to each other on the outdoor table and slowly, a part of an image appeared. He was baffled.

He continued to link more and more butts and finally a full picture emerged. Suddenly, the sun rose from behind while he was bending over his unfolding artwork. Birds were melodically chirping at that exact moment. All around him, the inmates were dazzled by this incredible talent in real time.

With a hard squint, Nicolas could recognise Donald Trump in the image. It was fascinating. He knew right then that this was his call from above. This was his mission in life. His idol was staring right back at him, and he heard him whisper that he should follow his heart in this endeavour. No sooner said than done, he fully embraced his newly discovered talent and created all sorts of images with used cigarette butts. Gorillas, camels, donkeys, birds, cats, coffins, presidents, you name it, Nicolas could create it. His artwork was displayed in numerous venues, including the main train station in Luxembourg city.

His imagination was limitless. He did not want to restrict his creative flow and just allowed his hands to align the butts in concordance with his heart. His ultimate plan was to fetch all the butts in the world and advise smokers not to throw them on the floor. He consequently named his art exhibitions 'not on the floor'. Obviously. His five children were amazed by their father's novel talent and so, they became his personal managers to promote his artwork all around the world, to the point of jointly publishing a book about it.

I fully understood then, that actually, I originate from a family of artists. It all finally made sense. Writers, movie directors and now more recently, a Cigarette-butt-aligning-Trump-producing-image-planet-saviour. There are simply no coincidences in life, I thought to myself, with a distinct face palm.

Following his premature liberation from prison a few years ago, Nicolas returned to live with his wife in the haunted house. The house, where the unimaginable happened day in, day out over decades. The tragedies, that the walls of that house have witnessed can't be undone. The song by Janie, presented in the early pages fits perfectly. The flair of the crimes still impregnated in these walls, that house will never be able to fully detoxify itself.

No amount of bleach in the world, would ever be sufficient to cleanse the memory of these walls. If they really had ears, how could they not hear the innumerable desperate cries for help from both mother and daughter? Whoever buys this house will, sooner or later, learn about the past crimes. Luxembourg is small. People talk. I have often taken my car, purposely driving to the few houses we lived in when I was a child. The house in Remich looks deserted. It doesn't look inhabited, and the greenery is totally out of control. That house most certainly looks like a haunted house. Who knows why it is unoccupied, perhaps people have been talking?

Back in his family, Nicolas was surrounded by his five children, who were ecstatic and relieved to have him back in their arms after the few, and in their eyes, unfair years, behind bars. Nicolas kept his family, and whoever was interested in hearing it, in the strong belief that he was sent to prison by God to guide the inmates to the right path. Needless to say, his family fully believed his words. There was not a single doubt in their mind that their beloved father had been innocent all along and that I was crazy like my mother.

Since he was hailed as the great artist by his children, Nicolas was given the opportunity to debut his actor career in the movie *Sawah*, directed by his son. Seemingly, Andreas could not find a better match to play the role of the loving and caring father of the protagonist in that movie. There seemed to be a shortage of male septuagenarians on the market.

In an attempt to restore his father's image after his release from prison, the film director gave his genitor a platform with no consideration of the trauma that this move may have on his own sister. Funded by millions of euros of public funds, the movie went on to be shown on *Netflix*. Andreas 'accidentally' omitted to mention to the funding board and the producers, that his father is a criminal and that publicly endorsing him may cause an uproar after the movie is made public. Not to mention, that the film was released when I was in the middle of heavy chemotherapy. The trauma being therefore even more amplified in my vulnerable state. The film director will therefore need to take responsibility for his actions and answer the ethical question of whether specifically choosing a convicted child molester to play the caring father role in a movie was a wise decision?

By not mentioning that rather deal-breaking detail to the funding body or the production company, Andreas has not only thrown a bad light on the industry but has also discredited himself for any future collaborations based on sincerity and accuracy. For me as a victim of that criminal, this provocative move was seriously a punch in the face. Andreas has yet again, tried to show me that I 'lost' after being humiliated for years in a heavy criminal trial that drew much media attention. He had recently been allocated another three million euros of public money for another movie, called *Hooped*.

In an interview, Andreas says that he wants to portray 'a painful period' in his life and show how his father has sacrificed so much for his family. Just reading that, makes me want to vomit. The sacrifice, that Andreas is talking about, is again proof of the false worldview that his father indoctrinated into him from a young age. Just like the other siblings, he also has repressed memories in a locked-up drawer in his mind, that only he can process by consulting a psychotherapist. Nobody can do that for him.

Hearing the revolting details of the abuse over years did not in any way soften Andreas' heart towards his little sister. The stocked-up jealousy since childhood has forever grudged him to the point of disconnecting him completely from reality. By publicly showing loyalty for his father, he sends an overt sign to all the abusers out there; that they can destroy their victim's lives and yet the repercussions are mild. One can even pursue an acting career using taxpayers' money. It goes without saying, that I could not watch the scenes in *Sawah*, in which my abuser was shown. Anything related to him still feels disgusting and will forever be. His eyes, his face, his voice, his laugh, his smell, his writing, his walk, are all nauseating to me.

By some strange coincidence, I mentioned *Sawah* to another lawyer, who was sitting in a meeting with my regular lawyer. This other lawyer, who himself, advocates for victims of sexual abuse, took this affair to heart and has managed to get the funding body to first suspend, and later convince the producers of *Hooped* to abandon the project. It is honestly very surreal to have got this result. I still believe in the ultimate justice, and this is just the tip of the iceberg.

This clear standpoint of society, openly condemning these crimes, soothes my heart. I also received a sincere apology from the producers of *Sawah*, which I can just qualify as healing. Despite me never getting a confession or apology from the actual criminal, the mere fact of having my pain acknowledged is indescribable. For me, and for all the other victims, for whom I have been a voice for over the past two years now.

Following the press release by the producers of *Sawah*, in which they describe in detail how Andreas glorified his father during the shooting of the movie and beyond, they both embarked on a revenge campaign against me. I was already used to the never-ending cyber-attacks that they initiated against me since the release of *Cruelly betrayed* in 2021, but this latest attack has deeply hurt me. They created social media accounts with my photo and name with the sole aim of mocking me. Beside the public humiliation, they have openly made fun of the sexual abuse, for which the abuser received a fifteen-year prison sentence. It shocked me to see, what they were capable of, how 'fearless' they were to not realise that identity theft was not the smartest idea.

Since the posted videos were part of the criminal investigation and in no way retrievable by a third party, how did they not anticipate that they would be caught?

Just a few days later, I was made aware that Nicolas

sent defamatory letters to multiple institutions, including my current employer. This was a deja-vu from 2009, when he sent letters from prison to every person who was dealing with me personally and professionally, to ruin my reputation. Back then, the judge forced him to write another follow-up letter, in which he stated that everything he had said about me was false. She also made him write me an apology letter, which he did, against his will. In a desperate attempt, Nicolas has portrayed me again, fourteen years later, despite an official conviction, as a cheating, lying, greedy, mentally unstable woman. He also wrote to the university I graduated from, that they must revoke my Master's degree and PhD. He concludes his long letter by urging the dean of the faculty to use his *alarming voice* to warn me that I must change my behaviour, come back to reality and respect human dignity.

It is not my word against his word. That ship sailed a long time ago. I do not need to prove that the abuse really happened. It is written black on white in a 100-page court judgement and was discussed over four painful years of investigations and trials.

Fourteen years later, I should not be spending energy, time, and money to still justify that this man has really done what he was convicted of by several judges. However, these recent attacks simply demonstrate what a victim still must endure, when she dares to speak up, press charges and defend herself. They show why these crimes mostly remain underreported. They confirm that the psychological and physical repercussions are lifelong. If a man, who is still out on probation, with a strict condition of not approaching his victim, dares to sign such letters with his actual name, it sends the message to me that he is at a point of no return. What is he able to do in real life to hurt me? The system must keep a close eye on this dangerous man.

In the middle of the Covid-19 pandemic in 2020, both, my mother and I received our cancer diagnosis. I was not too sure what to think of this synchronicity. Both our hells starting together in 1992 and both of us receiving a cancer diagnosis 28 years later. Then I receive the infamous call announcing her death, two hours following the good news that my scan was clear. Body and mind can't be separated. The chronic increase of stress hormones, namely cortisol and adrenaline in the system has an inverse relationship with the immune response.

If these stress hormones are constantly elevated, the immune response is chronically weakened. Adding insomnia to the mix sees that the body never gets the opportunity to relax. The correlation between psychological stress and physical debilitation is very well recognised. There is no denial that a distressing psychological state, acute and/or chronic can induce somatic conditions. Moreover, the causal link between childhood trauma and pathologies in adulthood, such as autoimmune, cardiovascular, respiratory, metabolic and cancer is very well acknowledged.

It is not a coincidence that my mother also received a cancer diagnosis. As mentioned, the intense chronic stress that she was subjected to over the past decades caused her body to finally say STOP. Similarly, my state of perpetual stress, chronically because of the PTSD from the abuse but also acutely, due to the chaos initiated by Felix, also broke me physically in the end.

Both my mother and I didn't have a genetic contributing factor for our cancer, it was purely immune-dependent and therefore 100 % stress-induced. One can have a genetic predisposition and never get cancer. One can have no genetic predisposition and get cancer. Ultimately, the environment will be the trigger as to whether a person will be affected or not. Studies are often done with identical twins who have the same genetic make-up and therefore the same risks of being affected by certain conditions, based on genetic mutations or variants. However, the observation that one twin ends up getting a disease and the other not is often explained by their different environments. They could be living in different corners of the world, entertain different lifestyles or be exposed to different stress levels.

Since I got hold of all her medical archives, I could see what happened to my mother, documented in great detail. It all started with a local, slow growing, non-aggressive, harmless hormone-positive tumour.

A very curable breast cancer, not even requiring chemo-, radiotherapy or surgery as a treatment.

It could have been cured by the intake of an anti-hormonal treatment in the form of daily pills. That's when the incredible journey started, which I have trouble understanding until this day. On the other hand, my cancer was very aggressive, fast growing, incurable and in theory, she should have been the one to have easily survived hers, while I should have been six feet under since 2020.

The initial diagnosis was not believed by the family. When I say family, I mean her husband and her five other children. I was fully out of the loop and only knew the details after her death. The family insisted that she only had an infection and should be treated with antibiotics, despite every clinical document time and time again stating in black on white that it, in fact, is cancer. Let's not forget that most of these people are medically trained and should have pretty much understood what the situation was. Fully dependent on these six family members, she was taken from doctor to doctor, in the hope of finding 'answers' to the worsening symptoms, thereby letting the tumour grow and grow without medical interference.

A few months on, the tumour had already spread to surrounding areas. At this point, my mother would not have been able to only have pills, but she urgently needed chemotherapy/radiotherapy and/or surgery to cure this common, curable cancer. Once again, the family refused her any treatment. We are now seven months after the initial diagnosis and my mother is kept under the strong belief that she has an infection, which is supposedly causing the pain. She is still being given strong psychiatric medication, resulting in her being totally disconnected from reality and not realising how severe her condition is and how she will soon die without appropriate cancer therapy.

Since I had no idea what she was going through and I had not talked to her since 2009, I had no way of knowing her situation except through the few updates that my abuser's probation officer was giving me. They usually went like this 'Nicolas is adamant that your mother has no cancer, and it is just an infection; He asked me to tell you to stop mentioning cancer'. I have regularly harassed my siblings to finally give our mother cancer treatment and repeatedly told them that they will have blood on their hands after she dies. It was evident that she was going to die, surrounded by my careless siblings, blindly obeying their guru.

When I was going through a heavy chemotherapy myself end of 2020, I took all my courage and called my mother after a decade of not speaking and that's when she told me that she had cancer. Despite knowing that she has cancer and receiving an antibiotic for it, she didn't seem too fazed by the severity of it. No surprise there, the antipsychotics were fully numbing her from feeling any emotion. She was totally at the mercy of Nicolas, Andreas, Denise, Leonard, Elena and Mira. She had no chance. If they say it's only an infection, then it must be, right? Let's remind ourselves, that my mother was a doctor and knew very well what it meant to have cancer.

She was left suffering, the cancer spreading more and more throughout her body over the months. The pain that accompanies this natural progression of the disease is excruciating and no human in their right mind would bear watching this without interfering to relieve the pain for the patient, in this case, your own wife and mother. How this could happen is utterly criminal. The pages reveal the horrors that unfolded over the months since the initial diagnosis in 2020. A few doctors' letters acknowledge the sadness at this patient's situation and the disbelief that the family could be in such denial with regards to the cancer despite there being more than enough evidence to confirm the diagnosis.

In another report, the oncologist describes how the husband is fully speaking on the patient's behalf and that according to him, the 'problem' in the breast started in 1983, when his daughter Mary was born. Apparently, she bit her mother's left nipple until it bled, and this wound had never healed over the following 40 years, which has now caused this 'problem'.

How does a specialist keep a straight face listening to this nonsense? So, apparently, I am fully responsible for my mother's death, because I bit her during breastfeeding 40 years ago. What makes me sad in this story, is that my mother may have believed this stupid theory Nicolas came up with. I wouldn't be surprised how she would take everything he told her at face value, with all the medication she was under.

In another account, my mother was told by the doctor that she had cancer and she broke down crying, shocked by the diagnosis. It's as if she had heard it for the first time although she had had the diagnosis for a few months at that point. Perhaps in her most lucid moments, she realised that what was happening to her was severe. Yet, she had no will of her own. If her family was refusing her treatment, that's what would happen. The doctors could not force any cancer treatment if her family was not going to give their consent. Again and again, the records were stating that she was unable to give consent and that she was not aware of her diagnosis, treatment, and prognosis due to her *psychiatric condition* requiring her to stay on antipsychotics.

In an interview with Mira, the medical staff in the UK tried to understand the social background of the patient. Mira starts off by saying that our mother had an arranged marriage with another man than the fiancé that she loved. Mira then says that her mother did not have a life, no friends or family. She spent her life watching TV. According to Mira, her mother has seven children (?). She says that her mother is not in good terms with her husband and that there is no element of abuse at home. She believes, however, that her mother holds a grudge against her husband and that is why, she refers to him as 'ex-husband'. Mira says that she is not willing to talk about the past as it stresses her out too much and that the nurse should ask the other sister, who lives in the North of England, to speak to her.

There seemed to be an ongoing disagreement between my mother and father. On the one hand, Nicolas was trying to convince medical staff that his wife was deceiving them. On the other hand, my mother was attempting to convince medical staff to keep every information about her from her husband. Despite the powerful medication, my mother had never ceased to advocate for herself and always tried to show what an abusive husband she had, in the hope of finally being rescued, to no avail.

As her situation was getting worse by the month, my father decided to move her to the UK in an apartment on her own, without any medical care at all. She was slowly being eaten up from the inside by her cancer and was left alone in a foreign country away from home. Her destiny was written and there was nothing any external person could do to interfere with the puppeteer, pulling the strings as he saw fit. Two years on from the initial diagnosis, the pages describe how my mother was experiencing all the symptoms that go along with a cancer left to run its natural course.

She was mercilessly being invaded by a very curable cancer, only because others decided that she had no cancer but only an 'infection' and fully made her believe this. Evidently, when the cancer became advanced enough, there was no way, Nicolas could continue hiding her in that apartment and had to bring her to the hospital where her hell continued and finally caused her death.

The guru and his five followers kept calling or even showed up in person at the hospital, adamant that the doctors and nurses were the ones who had made our mother sick. They threatened with legal action and insisted our mother be given random medication. Medication that they thought were THE cure to the cancer, which they still denied until my mother's last breath. The 'medical advice' that my family was giving the professionals was very illogical and counterproductive. They would only have accelerated my mother's death if the medical staff had listened to them.

Obviously, without knowing any context to this mad family, the doctors and nurses were at their wits' end. They most likely assumed it was a cultural influence rather than a perverted, utterly sick sect, ultimately provoking my dear mother to die. Having blood on one's hands is an understatement when considering the gravity of what happened.

No matter how I turn it, there is absolutely no possible justification in my mind for letting that cancer evolve as it did over two years despite the diagnosis being repeatedly confirmed of a curable harmless cancer.

The documents describing my mother's preventable deterioration are heart-wrenching. I could barely read them all. Ten days after my mother's passing, my abuser started a legal battle with me. Thirteen years after the first time he found himself jailed after I pressed charges. He may still not understand who he is dealing with but the audacity to dare to send me obnoxious letters from his lawyer via a bailiff, threatening me is incredible to say the least.

Along with his five beloved children, typing the nonsense he dictates to them, without ever questioning the ethics, they have all embarked on a mission of vengeance against me. Fuelled by the same sick energy as fourteen years ago, they have not evolved. On the contrary, they have accumulated more and more intense grudge against me and have no shame to publicly show their adoration for their father. Seriously threatening my lawyer, Nicolas seemingly had nothing to lose anymore.

During the ongoing legal battle, Andreas published a very sad announcement as to how Luxembourg is not taking care of its elderly population while leaving his dear father in a bad situation due to the increasing electricity and gas costs. This public post was linking an equally 'heart-breaking' *GoFundMe* page of my abuser himself, pleading in a long letter how a certain 'person' is making his life difficult. In his text, he describes my mother's last moments before her death in gory details. Andreas also publicly blamed the health system in the UK as well as Brexit for failing his mother and that she had to 'pay' the price with her life.

Nicolas, in his *GoFundMe*, says that he moved my mother to the UK because he had no idea why her arm was swelling and that he needed to see other medical options than Luxembourg. What a hypocrite to speak about a 'medical error' when one knows what truly happened over the past two years with my mother.

Often, when people are at the end of their lives, they become their real self. I have experienced that first hand when I had nothing else to lose, waking up from a long and complicated surgery, only to be told that my cancer had spread. At that moment, people often adopt the ultimate 'not give a continental' attitude. This allows them to be true to themselves without society's codes. Many times, people who are dying, spurt out their deepest regrets or even their gravest sins. It's like they want to 'vomit' everything out before dying. They don't want to be buried with their truth.

In this context, my mother showed her absolute disgust and hatred towards her husband and told the team that she never wants to see this man again. She told them that he must not be given medical information about her, and she was very distressed when she was asked about him. It's like she knew she was dying and had to show one last time how this monster destroyed her life, until the bitter end.

Shortly before my mother's passing, Nicolas is said to have been frustrated and still maintained that his wife did not have cancer, despite all the factual evidence at hand. He said that the team made a clinical error and insisted that everyone was against his wife. That same day, Denise was also on the phone, aggressively questioning the cancer diagnosis and insisted that the medical staff was incompetent.

On her death bed, my younger sister Elena made my mother sign a contract to sell her house. The nurse questioned this act when she saw that my mother signed without reading the text. She was suspecting abuse of trust and therefore asked my mother what the content of these papers were. My mother could not answer and said that she fully trusts her daughter. In the records, it is also noted how 'the husband' always spoke for his wife and did not understand nor respect the patient's capacity and choice.

One must admit that it is quite striking how 'the husband' plays the biggest role in the thousands of pages of medical records of the past thirty years from seven different hospitals. He had been controlling the narrative all along, without too much restraint, feeling outright powerful.

Recently, amid a dirty trial that he initiated against me, Nicolas has dared trying to get in contact with my children behind my back, luring them with presents, supposedly coming from their dead grandmother. This man has no limits and so, I put in place all the safety measures that can give me peace of mind that my children and myself are safe, no matter the cost.

Chapter Ten

My Verdict

With all the evidence at hand, there is no doubt that Nicolas is not only a man holding immoral values and beliefs but he's also a dangerous member of society and for the greater good, needs to be locked up behind bars; never to be let out again. He has continued to cause suffering all around him and will not stop until he is forcefully made to. This man should never have set foot back in society after being released from prison sooner than expected. The justice system in Luxembourg should keep a close eye on him as he has shown no remorse despite decades worth of evidence filled with cruelties perpetrated by him and his five children.

A recent letter sent by his lawyer says it all and shows how one can construct a new narrative based on pure lies and nonchalantly disregard glaring proof leading to an official conviction of a criminal. This was only a few weeks following my mother's death. An extract of the letter is shown below to show what a victim of tens of years of agony must still deal with, even so many years later. I am shocked that this is an actual official lawyer's letter and not simply someone's opinion.

...As I understand she has also written a book about **certain imaginary sexual experiences that she wrongly believes, in her own mind, that they had occurred by her own father** *a long time ago, abusing unjustly, unfairly and squarely not only her own father but also her deceased mother and, as a result, distancing herself from all her family members, thus causing great distress to them all and, no doubt, feeling very bad and distraught herself.*

...Only if she withdraws her published book and, **like a good Christian, shows remorse and amends her outlook** *of all her above-mentioned relatives will she, probably, be forgiven and be welcomed back into her family again.*

I had heard this sentence before, quite extensively during the four years of investigations and trials. I should show remorse and, like a good Christian, confess in Church for what I DID to my father and then I will hopefully be forgiven and be allowed back in the family. No wonder many victims never dare to speak up, especially if the abuser is a close family member or family friend. It takes a lot of courage to escape such a sect-like construct without ever looking back.

The psychological manipulation is very difficult to decipher, especially if it begins in childhood. As often, when a sect member leaves the sect, the 'rejected' member, does not only experience the repercussions by the guru, but his followers join in too. They will quickly go from victims to perpetrators once the honour of their leader is shaken. My siblings would die for their father, as stated black on white in emails sent to the police, when he first got arrested.

Be it 5 years or 15 years later, the denial of the obvious truth by my family is shocking. What would these people need to experience for them to realise what they have been accomplices to for all these years? Will they wake up one day and understand who really has been pulling their strings all their life? It is impressive how one can be a highly educated member of society, responsible for other patients while on the other hand be this dangerous in denying the undeniable. It is easier to reject one person than reject the image of the perfect family. It is easier to believe that the father is almighty and pure rather than look him in the eyes and see the child molester that he really is.

How can they put their grandchildren on his lap after hearing disgusting details for over four years about what he has done to their own sister. The loyalty these children show their father, despite being adults by now is crazy to say the least. When will they wake up? Will they ever? Perhaps his death will be THE ultimate trigger to release themselves from his grip.
He has been controlling them since childhood and in a way, they are also victims but somehow, I can't bear to hear that excuse anymore. My siblings have repeatedly helped Nicolas, falsify my mother's and my signature on official documents to cash in money from the government in our names, without questioning any wrongdoing. Nicolas always manages to justify

any immoral act to them. They remain his mindless pawns, that he can move as he sees fit.

I first pressed charges in 2009 and if they have been stuck in that same mindset for this long, I feel minimal hope for them to be able to wake up from their trance of denial. It will be very difficult for them to take a step back and look at the facts with an objective view. That train has left the station, maybe for good. Living a total lie is more comfortable than looking the truth in the eyes and feeling the pain that comes with finally facing one's childhood trauma.

They will need extensive therapy to deal with their own heavy past. Despite not being molested themselves, they have also witnessed the suffering our father made our mother endure. They have also been to the same cold and grey psychiatric hospital and their childhood foundations have also been extremely unhealthy. This may be contributing to them holding onto the 'perfect family' image constructed by their father. They also didn't have any other reference person to rely on and therefore his truth was the only truth.

I have been in therapy for years now and believe that this should be normalised. There is a huge taboo around seeing a psychotherapist. It is life essential as one can't make sense of all these emotions without a professional point of view on them. In essence, the parents mess up the upbringing of their children, after which, their adult children end up in lifelong therapy, attempting to understand and fix their parents' failings. Nicolas has destroyed lives, not only mine and my mother's but also my siblings', they just don't know it. They still hail him as God's son sent from Heaven to save humanity. They have repeatedly said that me pressing charges in 2009 has ruined their lives, without blaming their father at all.

That step to the psychologist's practice is mostly a conscious decision and unless one is prepared to face their trauma, they will not grow any further. Instead, their life will be defined by what happened to them as children. If they choose not to deal with it and prefer to sweep it under the carpet, then they will unconsciously pass their insecurities and fears to their children. This intergenerational trauma cascade will not end until one generation is ready to face the suffering from the trauma that is not theirs to start with.

Over the past years, my siblings have attempted to reach out to me, as they like to call it to start a 'dialogue'. The latest one came from Andreas, coincidentally it was a few days before the newspaper report was meant to be released about how he glorified his father using public funds. Thankfully, I can now see through the opportunistic intentions and not fall for these empty initiatives. In my kindness and perhaps, my wish to have something like a 'family', I have often fallen for these 'dialogue' requests, not knowing that they were orchestrated by my abuser. I am pretty sure that my siblings deeply believe what they have been told about me since our childhood. They are convinced that I am mentally deranged and naïve.

They have ganged up against me for the past 30 odd years, why wouldn't it work now, they thought. Before, during and after the criminal trial, I was left alone, with no family support, extended family included. Despite the family being quite large, no cousins, aunts or uncles have approached me until today. I believe I still have a grandmother in Canada. Radio silence. Why am I not surprised?

A few years ago, Leonard emailed me his grief. He started off gently by wishing me a happy birthday, then showed his real face and let everything out. He said that he realises the reasons why I did the things I did and that he doesn't blame me. He then continued by stating that I was not a monster to him. He just wanted *to patch things up*. Apparently, everybody wants me back in the family, *we all love you*. He then went off on a rant and said that I was a liar and that I will go to prison. He said that he now finally had the ultimate proof that I had been lying during the four years of investigations and trials and that now, he would expose me.

He told me to say goodbye to my children as they will be growing up without a mother, since I'll spend the rest of my life in prison. *Because of you and your nonsense with the trial, I have been a virgin all my life; I have never been on a date, and you ruined my life!* Then, he compared himself to Jesus, who also unfairly suffered like he did. He begged me to stop and explained that he can keep me away from prison; I just needed to trust him.

He continued his plead by telling me how I should proceed. First, I should write an apology letter to our father and never ever see him again. *I really mean it.* Then I must tell the judge that I no longer fear any consequence from him or my family. He told me that I lost my chance to be his daughter; *that ship has sailed.* He then promised and gave me his guarantee that I will walk free. I will not have to pay back anything, and in fact, he shall give my children a fund for university once he lands his first business deal. He then told me that his words are legally binding and that I can take this to a lawyer and sue him in the future if he doesn't keep his promise. He assured me that he is well connected and can help me if I fear legal trouble.

To finish off, he threatened me that if I don't do what he says and I *continue my story that hasn't even got one leg to stand on,* that he can tell me with high certainty that people will find out the truth once he becomes famous. He then concluded by saying that I will be the one crucified, spending the maximum sentence in prison; and that nobody cares about me. It is now my choice as he had hard evidence to back everything up. This chapter could end within my comfort zone or could drag me through hell at a later time. *Maybe in one month, maybe a year. I hope you understand. Yours sincerely, Leonard,* signing off his letter as if he was talking business.

When referring to my upbringing, I can barely say 'in our family' - 'in our sect' sounds significantly more accurate. Naturally, I have envied people around me and honestly still do. I often wonder how it would have felt to grow up in an intact family. It is not always easy to dissociate from this deep rooted brainwashing. By dissecting this criminal and changing my perspective, I realise, that actually, this man who's had me in the belief that I am worth nothing, stealing my dignity in the process, is an absolute loser.

I refuse to let this loser have the upper hand over my fate. I claim my life back. I will not give him the satisfaction of having destroyed me. The best revenge is my happiness. The best revenge is me moving forward and exposing that criminal for what he actually is; a pathetic being, full of insecurities, who needs to prey on innocent children to feel alive.

I speak for all the children and inner children of adults who were abused as a child or teen and have been silenced for too long. As a society, we must take a clear stand. For all these children, for all these adults who have gone through the sieve, when they needed love and protection as children. We have enabled their abuse to continue, by our inaction and our ignorance.

Now that we clearly know that these atrocities are happening all around us to the most vulnerable people in our society, we are to blame by not condemning it and by not educating ourselves about the topic. These are rarely isolated cases, they concern all of us. It is not an 'issue' between the abuser and their victim. Let's do it for all of them. For all these children that we as a society have failed to protect. For all these broken adults that we as a society have failed to save. Let's show them that the guilt and shame truly belongs to the abuser and not the victim by speaking up about it.

With regards to the reinsertion into society after being convicted for these heavy crimes, strict and serious conditions need to be part of the deal. The obvious condition is to be forced to have therapy to prevent him or her from inappropriately touching another child ever again. The other limitation should be to never be allowed to work or be around children. A person, who was able to sexually abuse a child has somehow been able to cross an unthinkable barrier. With all optimism I can scrape together, I will never be convinced that a child molester can fully be 'cured'. A convicted abuser, who has served his sentence for his wrongdoing, will need to confess and apologise to his victim(s) as this step undoubtedly contributes to the healing from the atrocities that only the criminal is responsible for.

Importantly, the lifelong psychotherapy that the victim needs to be having solely due to the perverted actions of the criminal, must be fully paid for by the abuser. That is the minimum of conditions, under which, in my eyes, a rehabilitation into society can be initiated. If the criminal is convinced that he has done nothing wrong despite hard evidence, then I am afraid, the chances of a successful reinsertion into society are very low.

Pedophiles, who think but not act out their impulses need structures to enable them to receive help. Most of them hate themselves for thinking and feeling this perverted attraction towards children. As a society, we must not condemn them but allow them to seek the appropriate help to never ever act upon their impulses behind closed doors. Remove the stigmatisation by not pointing fingers at them. The ones that have crossed the boundaries and have acted upon their impulses will need to treat themselves, whatever it takes to never ever repeat these crimes. Be that psychotherapy, medication, castration, sequestration, whatever is needed to protect their current or new victims.

Most cases will, however, remain undisclosed and the criminal will carry on unpunished for good, while the victim will be suffering for life, long after the crime has occurred. According to the Council of Europe, one in five children is subjected to sexual violence, more often girls than boys. That's 2-3 children per class and this may even still be an underestimation. Many critics will argue those numbers. In response, the Council of Europe has issued a press release stating that *the estimated figure of ONE in FIVE emerges from a combination of the results of various studies undertaken by research teams across Europe, and coincides with statistics advanced by Unicef, the International Labour Organization and the World Health Organization.*

ONE in FIVE is a regional European-level figure, but it

does not exclude that prevalence in individual countries may be higher or lower. Research in countries outside of Europe, such as in the United States and Canada, seem to reveal a similar level of prevalence.

The Council of Europe emphasises that it is very difficult to obtain a clear picture of the real situation because of underreporting, inconsistent methodologies and definitions in different studies, ethical issues, lack of procedural guidelines and tools to report sexual violence against children as well as the inability for children to reveal the abuse. Therefore many studies are based on interviews with adults, who were abused in their childhood or youth. There also seems to be a lack of effort invested in obtaining comprehensive, comparable data.

The figure ONE in FIVE refers to all forms of sexual violence against children: sexual abuse, child sexual abuse material, sollicitation of children through the Internet, child sexual exploitation and corruption of children. But because most available research refers only to sexual abuse involving physical contact, the **figure ONE in FIVE may actually be underestimated***, given the increase in sollicitation and exposure of children to pornographic material through the Internet.*

The lack of numbers, showing the real extent of these crimes against children has devastating consequences as this results in poor prevention strategies. It is a vicious circle really and millions of children continue to suffer as a result. I was not protected as a child, despite the obvious alarming signals, over and over again.

Even the government itself has failed me. ELEVEN reminders over a few years to conduct a social enquiry into my family home left me at the hands of my criminal, resulting in 16 years of horrors, while my hell could have been stopped after 'only' 4 years, had civil servants done their job properly. My rage at the injustice of it all, makes me want to do everything I can to protect these innocent children, because I very well know what it feels like to be silenced and hurt behind closed doors by the people who are supposed to love and protect you.

Over 90 % of sexual abuse cases against children are perpetrated by a person the child knows from their circle of trust. There is a big misperception in society where people tend to think that a child molester is a dirty, disgusting man with a moustache, wearing a white wife-beater and who comes from a low socio-economic social class. The abusers are everywhere around us, through all the social classes. They can also, very probably, be a charismatic person in society with a good social and professional status, loved by everyone. The abuser will put a great deal of effort into making sure that his or her image is clean and they are often perceived as loving and caring. It is rather a kind father, a sweet teacher, a great big sister, a generous banker, a loving grandmother, a wonderful priest, a caring football trainer, or a committed piano teacher.

For the child, the abuser is not always an abuser. It is for perhaps 20 % of the time while 80 % of the time it is a wonderful, caring and loving person of trust. A child does not possess the maturity or perspective to realise that the abuse is abuse. In addition, the conflict of loyalty will cause total confusion for the child. The abuser loves them after all, right? But at the same time, he or she is doing something the child neither likes nor wants, but they say it's for their good, so they know best, right?

This misperception of what a child molester looks like is a huge hurdle when it comes to the prevention and eradication of these atrocities against innocent children. Society needs to understand that child molesters live happily amongst us, that child sexual abuse does not care about religion, socio-economic status, gender, ethnicity or age. It is all through society. Women are also child molesters, just like boys can also be victims.

As a society, we are quick to condemn the random child molester that makes it into the news. The comments of appalled men and women say it all. They call for castration and even give visual details on how this monster should be slowly tortured and killed. As with many other societal issues, society is very hypocritical. If the child speaks out, it will often be by accident, as the child is devoured by shame and guilt and will therefore rarely find the courage to reveal the abuse. Imagine these allegations are made public, however, this time, the bad guy is our kind neighbour, our sweet cousin, our lovely aunt, our wonderful priest or our own son or daughter. We then waste no time keeping it quiet and more often than not, side with the alleged abuser while condemning the victim and discrediting him or her as a money- and revenge-seeking liar. This time, the victim will not only be silenced and intimidated by the abuser, but also by the abuser's fanclub.

One of the strategies of the abuser is to build a strong support network over time so that if the abuse ever comes out, everyone will cry out: *No way, this child is lying, XX has always been good to us. I don't believe this for a second, the child has been manipulated by XYZ.* Since the other strategy during grooming is to isolate the child and give him or her exclusive attention, the victim will often have a hard time finding support within or outside the family.

The lack of effective prevention policies remains the main challenge. Nations remaining blind to these tragedies due to lack of reliable numbers is inexcusable. The estimate of ONE in FIVE by the Council of Europe is an effective baseline study tool to motivate governments, parliaments, professionals and parents to take urgent action, to prevent sexual violence, protect children and prosecute offenders. I am hopeful that one day there will be a NONE in FIVE estimate and that these crimes will be a dark thing of the past.

Just like we managed to control Covid-19 and

mobilised finances and efforts into combatting this global pandemic, let's tackle this silent pandemic with the same energy; to create a safer world, for generations to come. We will rarely see images on the news displaying people going out on the streets holding up protest signs up and chanting an anti-child sexual abuse slogan. As a society, we are definitely enablers and it is not a surprise that abusers feel absolute impunity, day in, day out, to commit their perverted crimes. They know that society does not side with the victim and so, these criminals, have an easy game. In rare cases, the victim is lucky enough and his or her case lands in front of judges. In even rarer cases, the criminal gets convicted with an official confirmation that he or she has committed the crime. Following the conviction, however, they will often never even see a prison from the inside.

Our laws are still heavily in favour of these criminals while the victims suffer a lifelong sentence for a crime they have not committed. A big paradigm shift is urgently needed in society and the little child in me, that had to suffer because of the system failing her, is pushing me to do whatever is in my power to speak up about this best kept secret of all time. I will not stop until a change in the *status quo* is achieved and the system starts siding with the real victims of these crimes.

As a small country we can create a distinct change and put into practice the needed actions. These can then serve as best practice for other nations to follow suit. The contact to policy makers is much easier in Luxembourg than in other countries and so, change can happen faster. Where there is a will, there is a way. Often, there is no will, and that will is often missing because of a lack of realisation of the extent of any societal issue. The lack of realisation is there because of a lack of numbers and the lack of numbers persists because this silent pandemic is widely underreported.

There is no PCR test that can detect it, no specific symptoms, no rapid tests. There is no fast check for child molesters before getting into contact with children, you can't read their perverted intentions off their faces. On the contrary, their faces often display the exact opposite image that society associates with a child molester, hence this misperception being a huge issue in advancing the cause in my eyes.

In April and November, the world raises awareness that child abuse in all its forms exists and that we should protect these little ones from harm. I dream of a world, in which these awareness campaigns cease to exist. I dream of a world, in which children can be children, in which they are not treated as inferior objects to adults. I dream of a world, in which people are treated with kindness and respect. I truly believe that this world exists. In my eyes, nothing is impossible, and my dream is not utopian. If we all commit to it with our collective conscience, we can change the world, for generations to come.

Miscellaneous public posts

A love letter to my body

Dear Body of Mine,

I feel the need to write a love letter to you today as I am filled with absolute pride, respect, admiration and gratitude towards you.

Contrary to what my book cover states, I do not feel betrayed by you anymore.

I have grown up hating you from that first night you were abused when you were still developing.

I was disgusted by you to the point of hurting you on purpose, blaming you for everything.

You have carried me through decades of horrendous pain and suffering and yet you always rebound stronger than before.

You have carried and delivered 5 beautiful children without complaining.

You have endured long complicated surgeries, undergone burning radiotherapy sessions and horrible chemotherapy cycles and yet you bounce back and allow me to live on.

You have been put under extreme stress over and over again, without moaning to me while you were never allowed to rest.

Your limits have been tested for days, weeks, months, years and decades, only for me to survive because you knew very well that I would survive, no alternative option to that.

I am forever thankful to you and vow to love and care for you as I always should have done.

I am sorry that I couldn't see your true value until now. You are the most precious asset in my life.

With everlasting love, Mary

There are no losers or winners when it comes to cancer.

With a diagnosis, you get catapulted from one day to the other without warning into this unknown horrible fearful parallel world of cancer.

It is a world filled with intense fear, anxiety, anger, hope, perseverance, disappointment, courage, even joy and mostly a drive for self discovery.

I have met extraordinary people during the past months. Young and older patients from all over the globe.

We all share the same small simple uncomplicated benign wish – we want to be 'allowed' to live on.

Many of us put a discount on our life expectancy and state we would be happy if we could only live XX more years to see our children graduate or get married.

We mostly 'live' on a renewable 3-month lease.

Once a piece of paper confirms that the check was OK, we return to our daily life until the next check.

The daily physical impact from the heavy treatment may be invisible to others while we look 'normal' on the outside.

The intense constant fear is omnipresent while we try to regain some sense of normality.

A simple casual symptom makes us jump with fear of a recurrence. It is the ultimate mind game.

Why am I being particularly reflective today?

My sweet friend Aneta has passed away today. She was only 39 and a beautiful mother to 2 young children

There are no losers or winners when it comes to cancer.

Winning or losing somehow implies that one is fighting/playing better than the other one and this is why one has won and the other one has lost.

This is simply not true when it comes to this horrible disease.

Each patient is unique, each cancer is unique and should be treated as such.

There is no 'one size fits all' when deciding on the best therapeutic approach.

Ultimately, luck is a big factor in the survival of cancer. One thing I know for sure is that my lovely friend has fought just as hard as I did and I am yet to meet someone who has not given everything in order to stay alive.

I am currently feeling a deep sense of survivor's guilt while I am lucky enough to play with my children and my friend will never be able to experience this again.

Life can be very cruel.

Be grateful for just being able to breathe today.

When you next feel like life is so unfair because COVID prevents you from playing tennis, getting a haircut or eating at a restaurant...Please remember that many people are living in that parallel world alongside with only one wish to see another day.

Not all disabilities are visible

Isn't society funny and so very paradoxical?
While going through any hardship (aka life's panoply of shits), society wants you to be 'positive', smile more, complain less…..but please not too positive.
Allow me to elaborate.

Not all disabilities are visible to the naked eye.

The list of conditions that are invisible yet debilitating on a daily basis is very very long.

Be it chronic pain, mental illness, Crohn's, Diabetes, Cancer etc… if your outside look does not match your inside shit, society has a very hard time giving you empathy, let alone a drop of pity.

Well, here's my little attempt to raise some awareness. If it makes only one person be a little kinder to that stranger in need of help despite looking 'fit' then my time is not wasted writing this text.

Speaking from experience, my outside look has never matched my inside shit and as most of you know, my life has basically been one gigantic pile of shit.
I have always looked 'fine' regardless of the hell I was going through. This latest cancer hell has definitely taken a toll on my young body.

From one day to the other, I have gone from a seemingly fit 37 year old to a hopeless patient with an incurable aggressive cancer.

With 10h of surgery, 18 chemotherapy sittings and 30 radiotherapy sessions, my poor body has been given one of the most toxic medical treatments known to mankind.
The daily handicaps from the heavy treatment along with the brutal menopause made my body go from 37 straight to 77.

Chemo or not, I always put make-up on, fake eyelashes, fake eyebrows, fake hair and life went on.
I used to go to chemo with a nice dress, painted fingernails and a big smile on my face despite the horrible hell I was going through.

I looked 'happier' than someone who seemingly had a carefree life so I didn't get the needed empathy, not even some pity.
I needed to recognise myself in the mirror and never accepted that I was 'sick'.

I didn't conform to what society expected to see of a cancer patient...so it can't be that bad, right?
Oh it was bad, it was absolute hell but society needs to understand that we are all different dealing with life's shits and it's not because someone looks 'fine' that they are not in pain.

Today, I still have daily physical handicaps due to the heavy treatment despite looking 'fit'.
My deep sense of gratitude to just be allowed to live after cancer makes me dedramatise my daily pains but they are there and are lifelong.

I have learnt to ask for help from random strangers despite being very independent all my life...hard pill to swallow, I admit.

Please society, look beyond the outside facade. It's not because the person is not in a wheelchair or hobbling around, that he or she is not suffering.
Just like the saying on a disabled parking goes: you want the parking spot? Then take the handicap too.

I am pretty sure nobody would want to swap the daily handicaps (along with the heavy cancer treatment and the horrible fear of recurrence) for the few advantages I receive.
Just be kind.

Glossary of Medical Terms

Adrenaline - A hormone secreted by the adrenal glands, also known as the 'fight-or flight hormone'. It is released, amongst others in response to a stressful threatening situation.

Anaesthetic – A drug or agent that produces a complete or partial loss of feeling.

Anti-psychotic drug – A type of drug used to treat symptoms of psychosis.

Auto-immune – A condition in which the body's immune system mistakes its own healthy tissues as foreign and attacks them.

Cardiovascular – Relating to the heart and blood vessels.

Chemotherapy - Chemical substances used to kill or slow the progression of cancer cells.

Clavicle – Collarbone

Cortisol - The body's primary stress hormone. It is released, amongst others, in response to threatening situations.

Crohn's disease – A condition in which the gastrointestinal tract is inflamed over a long period of time.

C-section – The delivery of a baby by making an opening in the mother's lower belly area.

Delirious – Unable to think or speak clearly because of fever or mental confusion.

Delusions – A false belief or judgment about external reality.

Epidural – An epidural is procedure used to relieve pain during labour and birth.

Extrapyramidal side-effects – Drug-induced movement disorders

Genetic predisposition – An increased chance that a person will develop a disease based on their genetic makeup.

Genetic mutations – A change to a gene's DNA sequence to produce something different.

Haldol – Haloperidol is a first-generation antipsychotic that is a commonly used drug worldwide to manage symptoms of schizophrenia.

Hallucinations – A false perception of objects or events involving your senses: sight, sound, smell, touch, and taste.

Immune response – The way the body defends itself against substances it sees as harmful or foreign.

Insomnia – A common sleep disorder that can make it hard to fall asleep, hard to stay asleep, or cause you to wake up too early and not be able to get back to sleep.

Metabolic – Relating to metabolism (the chemical processes within the body required for life)

Metastases - The development of secondary cancerous growth away from the primary cancer

Neuroleptic drugs – Drugs used to treat and manage symptoms of many psychiatric disorders.

Paranoid delusions – A symptom of psychosis. A person with psychosis will often believe an individual or organisation is making plans to hurt or kill them.

Parkinson's disease – A brain disorder that causes unintended or uncontrollable movements, such as shaking, stiffness, and difficulty with balance and coordination.

Port-a-catheter – A device that is usually placed under the skin in the right side of the chest to administer drugs such as chemotherapy.

Post-traumatic stress disorder (PTSD) – A disorder that develops in people who have experienced a shocking, scary, or dangerous event.

Radiotherapy - Cancer treatment using ionising radiation to kill cancer cells.

Respiratory – Relating to the organs that are involved in breathing.

Schizophrenia – A mental disorder characterized by disruptions in thought processes, perceptions, emotional responsiveness, and social interactions.

Somatic – Relating to the body, especially as distinct from the mind.

Spinal block – Drug-induced temporary loss of feeling in the abdomen and/or the lower part of the body.

Symptomatology – The set of symptoms characteristic of a medical condition or exhibited by a patient.

Tranquilisers – Drugs that calm and reduce stress and tension. Tranquilizers are used to treat anxiety and insomnia.

Useful Contacts

Author's contact: dr.mary.faltz@gmail.com

Website: www.maryfaltz.com
Facebook: Dr. Mary Faltz
Instagram: dr_mary_faltz
Linkedin: Mary Faltz, MPharm, PhD

Useful links and contacts (Luxembourg)

ALUPSE
www.alupse.lu
Tel: 26 18 48 1

BEE SECURE Stopline
www.stopline.bee-secure.lu
BEE SECURE Helpline
Tel: 26 64 05 44

Femmes en détresse
www.fed.lu
organisation@fed.lu

Child protection
www.childprotection.lu

ECPAT
www.ecpat.lu
ecpat-luxembourg@ecpat.lu

Kanner Jugend Telefon (KJT)
Tel: 116 111
www.kjt.lu

La Voix des Survivant-e-s
www.survivant-e-s.lu
lvds.lux@gmail.com

Ombudsman fir Kanner a Jugendlecher (OKAJU)
www.okaju.lu

Office national de l'enfance (ONE)
www.one.public.lu

Police grand-ducale 'Protection de la Jeunesse'
Tel: 12321

Service central d'assistance sociale (SCAS) - service d'aide aux victimes
Tel: 47 58 21 1

SOS Détresse
Tel: 45 45 45

Fondation Cancer
Tel: 45 30 331
fondation@cancer.lu

Centre de réhabilitation post oncologique du Château de Colpach
Tel: 27 55 43 00

Groupes Sportifs Oncologiques
info@sportifsoncologiques.lu
Tel: 691 12 12 07

Cérémonie des étoiles- Maternité G-D Charlotte
chl@chl. Lu

Thank you for leaving a review of this book online. If we all contribute to reaching a wider audience then we'll help raise awareness about childhood sexual abuse and empower others who find themselves facing adversity.

Printed in Great Britain
by Amazon